808.8 OS

O's little book of happiness

O's

Little Book of Happiness

O's

Little Book of Happiness

The Editors of *O, The Oprah Magazine*

FLATIRON
BOOKS
NEW YORK

O'S LITTLE BOOK OF HAPPINESS. Copyright © 2015 by Hearst Communications, Inc. All rights reserved. Printed in the United States of America. For information, address Flatiron Books, 175 Fifth Avenue, New York, N.Y. 10010.

www.flatironbooks.com

All material included in this book was previously published, in slightly different form, in *O, The Oprah Magazine*. *O, The Oprah Magazine* is a registered trademark of Harpo Print, LLC.

The Library of Congress Cataloging-in-Publication Data is available upon request.

ISBN 978-1-250-06856-9 (hardcover)
ISBN 978-1-250-06857-6 (e-book)

Flatiron books may be purchased for educational, business, or promotional use. For information on bulk purchases, please contact the Macmillan Corporate and Premium Sales Department at 1-800-221-7945, extension 5442, or write to specialmarkets@macmillan.com.

First Edition: March 2015

10 9 8 7 6 5 4 3 2 1

You can never be happy living someone else's dream.
Live your own. And you will for sure know
the meaning of happiness.

—OPRAH WINFREY

Contents

Simple Pleasures

Each moment in time we have it all,
even when we don't.

—MELODY BEATTIE

The Way Home

Christie Aschwanden

—✳—

The walk is not negotiable. No matter how full the day's agenda, we go—my husband, my cow dog, and I—down our rural western Colorado road, past the neighbor's property to the dead end, up the old dirt track grown over with sagebrush and piñon saplings, to the top of the hill where the path ends under a red sandstone cliff. I've watched sunset after sunset from this private perch, and each is the most beautiful I've ever seen.

As an air force brat, a competitive ski racer, and then a journalist, I've lived in three countries and more than a dozen cities; trekked up and down the Alps, through Central American rain forests, and along Mediterranean coasts, seeking novelty and adventure. But a kind of loneliness lurked in my perpetual motion. I could fit in anywhere, yet I belonged nowhere.

Seven years ago, I fell in love with Cedaredge, the small town where my husband, Dave, yearned to settle, and together we decided to put down roots on a sixteen-acre homestead. Still, I refused to retire my passport. There were so many faraway mountains to climb and foreign cultures to explore. Tying myself to a single place felt confining—until finally, during a particularly irritating flight delay, it dawned on me that while I wasted time in crowded airport lounges, the life I'd dreamed of was waiting for me on the farm.

Later that week, I told Dave that I would spend the next 365 days practicing the art of living in place, never venturing more than a hundred miles from home. It was my version of a Benedictine monk's vow of stability, in which he promises to remain in the same monastery for life, resolving to accept his assigned home as it is.

Although a part of me believed I was making a sacrifice, I found that when I narrowed my boundaries, I expanded my horizons. The friendship I forged with my octogenarian neighbors taught me that a shared commitment to place can create ties far stronger than age. Joining my library's board introduced me to bibliophiles I would have otherwise never met. And with a local activist whose politics make me cringe, I found common ground in our passion for growing raspberries.

But it was my dog who finally showed me the way home. Oskar inspired the ramble that would become our ritual. And after treading this little path for hundreds of days, I've stopped longing for far-flung adventures. Here I have the aroma of sage and the bluebirds and the craggy peaks surrounding me like an embrace. I share this space with the beings whose footprints I see in the mud—coyotes, turkeys, elk, and mountain lions—and my presence has turned me into a creature of the habitat just like them.

It has taken me most of my life to learn how to inhabit a place, and I learned it, finally, by walking—up the hill and around the back side of our farm, day in and day out. The repetition is the point. My journey home was not a whirlwind excursion but a geological process: my soul mingling with the soil, step by step, over time.

Lumps Are Treasures

Patricia Volk

—✳—

I love the dark film that forms as cocoa cools in the pot. Break it up with a spoon, stir it in, and you've got dirty hot chocolate, unsmooth and imperfect, hence complex. There are those who will tell you dirty food does little to enhance presentation. But a brisket sandwich would be torment without pan scrapings. I like seeing and eating something that shows it was made by human hand in a slow old-fashioned way. When I'm eating a lemon mousse, discovering a bit of pulp exhilarates. You never have to strain anything for me. Lumps are treasures, and so are little bits of black fat at the bottom of the roasting pan if onions are in it. In Yiddish, these carbonized fat-soaked threads are known as *gribenes*. People, families, have been known to fight over them. In France, burnt crumbs that collect at the bottom of the skillet when you sauté floured food is *fond*. *Gribenes* and *fond* are why we have Lipitor. Congealed anything, stuff that leaks between the bread and gets frazzled on the panini maker, hard bits, dried bits, soggy bits, crunch, globs, gobs, and flecks—anything you might toss even though it has more taste per concentrated morsel than the star of the meal—I say bring it on. There's a reason the word *incredible* contains the word *edible*.

Book Lust

Pamela Erens

—✳—

I've been a passionate reader since childhood. Print is beautiful to me. My eyes automatically seize on any text in the vicinity, whether a DANGER HIGH VOLTAGE sign or the side panel of a box of Cheerios. Some grown-ups remember the times they swam in a cold pond or raced their bikes along a country road as children. I remember going out to the beach one morning with *The Once and Future King* and looking up to find that the sun was setting. I remember the time I read *The Outsiders*, a book about disaffected teenagers, from cover to cover while draped upside down over a kitchen chair. My body hurt like hell, but I would have had to stop reading to get up.

I can't read with that level of absorption anymore. In

fact, during much of the day there are things I can't read at all. The newspaper, a book review, a lively magazine profile are all fine. But even when I have the luxury of complete solitude, I'm unable, before the hour of ten P.M., to read a novel or a reflective essay.

Only after the children have gone to bed, my husband and I have performed triage on our to-be-discussed list, and my schedule for the next day has been organized can I sink into language with a capital *L*. I get into bed, adjust my thin pillow against my fat pillow. I put on my socks (it's no fun reading with cold feet). I open my book, and the following thought allows me to begin: *No one needs me.* Maybe no one even remembers who I am! It's too late in the day for me to make any more mistakes, disappoint anyone, complete any uncompleted tasks. However I may have failed or fallen behind, I'm off the hook until sunrise. And time, which all day has pressed like a tight band against my consciousness, slackens. The clock finds a thirteenth hour.

Sometimes I do stalk my bookshelves in the middle of the afternoon during an unexpected windfall of free time, eyes scanning the unread novels, essay collections, ruminations on God and love and history—all the biggies. My heart beats rapidly; I grow excited with possibility. I'm in love with the many things that I have yet to feel and know. I'm experiencing the *idea* of reading, which is generally so stimulating that I discover I can't begin at all.

But when the bedroom light is dimmed and the tele-communicatory hum of the universe has been smothered behind the closet door, I'm ready for the *reality* of reading, which is less exalted but ultimately more satisfying. I find it in myself to begin; I open to page one. A man is standing in a bakery on a hot summer afternoon. I see the shirt the man is wearing, note the fact that his tie is folded in his pocket. I see the baker's wife at the cash register. Suddenly I'm sheltered by a thicket of detail. The sights and sounds and smells of the book pull me in and slow me down in a way that those of the real world, oddly, often do not. I'm no longer at the wishing-fearing-planning pace of my day. I'm not running but walking. And where I wind up, book after book, is an unmatched state of bliss.

Paradise:
Seventeen Cents a Spoonful

Mark Leyner

—✳—

Imagine condensing the evolution of gastronomic pleasure from the very first mammalian sip of mother's milk to everything savored and swallowed over the millennia into one single alimentary act. Sound crazy? If so, you've never had pudding. And, friends, I'm not talking about hot, steamy Christmas puddings, bread puddings, figgy puddings, crème brûlées, or zabagliones. I'm talking about the store-bought, ready-made pudding you find in the refrigerated section of your supermarket. I'm talking six plastic four-ounce cups of cold, thick, dizzyingly sweet pudding for around two dollars. I'm talking Swiss Miss. I'm talking Kozy Shack.

And actually, I've refined the act of pudding eating even

further, down to its Eucharistic essence—a single spoon-ful. Two ounces. Seventeen cents' worth.

Here's how it's done: Scoop out a tablespoon of pud-ding from the plastic container (butterscotch is regarded by pudding illuminati as the epitome of flavors), put it in your mouth, do not move it around or disperse it in any way with your tongue, swallow the glob intact, and let Mother Gravity slowly draw it down. Remember—this is as much about how it feels as it is about how it tastes.

Anticipation of that single sweet glob is the fuse that drives me through the day. A tablespoon of pudding is the perfectly titrated dose. It's a fugitive pleasure, swallowing a syllable. That sweet, thick syllable—*pudd*. The *-ing* is simply the slide down the throat, the *pudd* as it bids adieu. . . . The parting of the pudding is all sweet sorrow.

A cowboy's shot of whiskey in a saloon sends the cowboy west, far from Mama, toward trouble, exile, and ultimately into the sunset. But the spoonful of pudding has a completely opposite vector. It sends you back, back east, back to Mama, toward the dawn, all the way to Eden . . . before the fall of mankind. Paradise at only seventeen cents per glob! That's what I'm talking about.

Tall Tales

Victoria Redel

—✳—

Somewhere after Farson, Wyoming, my sons grew restless in the backseat. Who could blame them? We'd been traveling all day and well into the night, driving out of Utah to Thermopolis, Wyoming, home of the world's largest hot spring. "Just go to sleep," we commanded from the front seat, already exhausted by this vacation. "Tell us a story," they said—and so began the adventures of Extravaganza and her sidekick and more or less true love, Cowboy Pete. From that night on, they became part of all long family car trips.

Extravaganza rides her horse with a diamond tiara shining in the light of the moon. Or, hobo-style, she jumps trains to Detroit to win a few hands of cards while searching for the parents of a lost boy. Or she and Cowboy Pete crack treasure from a sunken lobster boat—they use the gold to help the lost boy, and the change is spent on strappy sandals. Our car rides are a means of going on vacation, of course—but now they've also become a way to go on a wild adventure, even when we're still strapped and buckled in.

A Slice of Summer

Abigail Thomas

—✳—

My grandmother lived in a big house on a ghost of a road at the end of which lay the Atlantic Ocean. Her house had once been an inn, was reputed to be haunted, and had been purchased for eleven thousand dollars in the late 1940s. Once a year, from wherever we were living—Baltimore, New Orleans, Minnesota—my family made the trek back for summer vacation. The place was always the same. Always the same bright green grass, the big gray front porch, the huge elms, flowering privet and roses and salty air, always the beach at the end of the road. Always summer.

At Bigmom's the smell of camphor and old books mingled with whatever was in the oven. There was always something good going on in her kitchen. The first thing I did when we arrived was run and look in her icebox. There (as I'd hoped) were glass ramekins filled with custard, each with a sprinkling of nutmeg. This silky treat was my favorite, and I was allowed to have two or even three in a row. Sometimes she made applesauce, hard green apples cut up and cooked in orange juice, which she pressed through a fine sieve. This thin, delicious substance was served with heavy cream. Her recipe for fudge, now lost, contained the instructions "Cook until the bubbles look as if they don't want to burst." My mother poured it over marshmallows. On the back of the old stove was a pot of broth, thick chunks of beef cooking with rice in water. Even though this was meant for Winston, the ancient, ailing English bulldog, I would stand at the stove and secretly eat spoonful after spoonful.

The earliest aroma of the day was Bigmom's coffee percolating at five thirty, and I tiptoed down the wide front stairs and into her kitchen, where I sat in the old rocker (now in my living room) and talked, about what I can't remember. For an hour, my grandmother was all mine. She let me have a cup of coffee with sugar and cream, and I felt alive with the possibilities of what life might be like for me. I guess this was because she appeared to take me seriously. Our coffee was accompanied by buttered toast cut into long strips she called soldiers.

When the rest of the household woke up, we kids went to the beach. We grew up there as much as anywhere, on that beach, in that water, stopping for lunch at noon, eating our chicken sandwiches—white meat, plenty of butter and salt, the crusts cut off the bread—or red onion sandwiches on tiny rounds of rye, hard-boiled eggs, everything eaten with the sand you could never quite keep off.

When the sun was over the yardarm, we trudged our sunburned selves back down Indian Wells Highway to her house. Interesting grown-ups were drinking their pink gins in the library; to the left was the parlor, filled with mysterious objects under glass domes and always as hushed as church. We'd race one another to the shower (her upstairs bathroom had a skylight with an old metal chain) and then back downstairs, avoiding the room where our parents were happily occupied. Our winter lives were harder. Schools and cities changed; almost as soon as we got settled somewhere, we were moving again. But summer was always summer.

My grandmother died and the house was sold, but for years and years afterward, whenever I returned to Amagansett, I felt at home. This was where I belonged. Anytime I walked down that half mile of road to find the ocean glittering at the end, I was a child.

Wind, Sand, and Sardines

Monica Ali

—✳—

One year I took the children on holiday to Morocco, where we spent much time feasting, either with our eyes in the market or with our bellies in the cafés and restaurants. One meal in particular marked a highlight. We were staying in Essaouira, a town with such an atmospheric and photogenic medina that it has remained a popular film location since Orson Welles chose to shoot there for his *Othello*. Setting out from the fishing harbor, we took a camel ride up the coast along vast deserted stretches of windswept golden sand, past the ruined forts and castles, which are said to have been the inspiration for the Jimi Hendrix song "Castles Made of Sand." Camel rides are notoriously uncomfortable, except this one wasn't—we lolled back on hugely overstuffed palanquins, going with the motion as if rolling with the waves. After a couple of hours we branched off at a small river and rode inland, seeing nothing but the occasional house and a few tree-climbing goats. When we stopped for lunch, our guide quickly swept together some leaves and twigs as kindling while the children collected bigger sticks. From somewhere in his saddlebags, he produced two dozen sardines, which he had caught that morning, and grilled them on the open fire. There was fresh bread and heavenly tomatoes. For dessert we ate dates. It was the simplest of meals and the most delicious. Why? It had been a long ride, for one thing. Food tastes better when you're hungry. How easy that is to forget! Everything was fresh and tasted of itself, no need for dressing up. And there was time for a doze beneath the acacias while the children fed the leftovers to the camels.

Personal Growth

Lara Kristin Herndon

—✳—

Two years ago, as my bitter divorce dragged on and on, I moved out of the high-rise apartment my ex and I had shared and into a small walk-up with our daughter. I felt like a shipwreck survivor—glad to have washed up on dry land, traumatized to be starting over from scratch.

A few days later, a package arrived. I opened it to find a beautiful green stalk sprouting several glossy emerald leaves. It was a lemon tree, a gift from my mother. My first thought: It was the dead of winter in Manhattan—how would I keep this thing alive? But caring for the little tree proved easy; all it needed was water and a warm windowsill.

When it blossomed—white waxy stars with sunshine

yellow centers whose sugar and honeysuckle scent my daughter and I gulped in by the lungful—our cramped apartment felt transformed.

The flowers dropped off in early March, leaving in their place tiny green lemons. In the months that followed all but one of those dropped off, too. The lone survivor grew and grew, bending the whole plant under its weight. We harvested our enormous lemon in August. It was sweet enough to eat whole, like an orange, but instead we made a small, delicious batch of lemonade that we drank on our stoop in the late-summer sun, both of us aglow with the singular exhilaration of starting fresh.

Bliss in Action

Happiness is not a station you arrive at,
but a manner of traveling.

—MARGARET LEE RUNBECK

My Blue Heaven

Anne Glusker

—✳—

It usually happens after the tenth lap. The weight of my body is released. Where it goes, I'm not sure—dispersed through that particular light blue-green of chlorinated pool seen through goggles, dissipated by the steady back-forth, back-forth of body through water. The first few laps are often dutiful, even agonizing. But when that lifting occurs, it's all suddenly different: I'm alone in my aquatic capsule, my carapace of skin. If all goes well—no one else too close ahead or on my heels behind—I become enmeshed in the water, no care, no worry. Body and mind, so often split, two alien entities, are, for at least this brief time, one.

For me, the world is too present in an aerobics class—the sight of the other people, the thump of the music. And

I never much wanted to *compete*, to chase a ball or be on a team. It's not that I'm a solitary person. On the contrary, I love people. Which is all the more reason to regularly disengage, to disappear from the hurly-burly of the world for a while.

Growing up, I enjoyed jumping waves in the ocean and an occasional swim in a bay, but nothing more. Then, in my late twenties, I became friends with a woman I later called Coach. She swam obsessively—a mile every night after work and on the weekends, too. She never made dinner plans for earlier than eight thirty because that's when she was finished at the pool. She probably got her lean, wiry body from her genetic code, but her toned shoulders and well-muscled arms could have come only from those endless chlorinated miles. I didn't understand her devotion until I accompanied her to the pool as a guest one day.

I was smitten. I loved the feeling of my arms pulling me along, the texture of the liquid all around me. I slowly acclimated to swimming culture—learning the lingo of length and lap, how many to a mile, how to use a kickboard, the way a flip turn improves your time. I never got terribly speedy or even approached Coach's diligence, but I did swim. I joined her pool, assembled my swim gear, bought a good pair of goggles. And when I did my first mile (thirty-six laps in most pools), I was inordinately proud. It sounded so grand: an entire mile. There was a ring of completeness to it, an aura of virtue.

Slowly, my arms developed a hint of muscle. I got my mile down to fifty minutes—a good time for a slowpoke like me. I settled into a schedule, sometimes doing just three-quarters of a mile, with half a mile as my bare minimum.

As I stroke up the lane, I count: one. On the way back I repeat: one. And I proceed from there: two-two. Three-three. Thoughts and ideas may crowd into my head, but they are all eventually banished by the slow, steady, rhythmic need to keep count. Four-four. Five-five. And soon, that amazing lifting sensation comes: the reward, when I take off and begin to flow.

Everything I Need to Know
I Learned from a Horse

Jane Smiley

—*—

A few days ago, I found a photo that was taken of me at forty-three sitting on my new horse (then fourteen). I look a little disheveled but happy; he looks thin, even emaciated, with very little tail and several scars where other horses have taken pieces out of his hide. What you can't tell from the photo, and what I didn't know at the time, was that the horse (whom I named Tick Tock, after the ticking of our biological clocks) was about to take me on a life-changing adventure that has been more fun, sometimes more troubling, and always more interesting than I could have possibly imagined.

I was a fearful person then, the sort who sneaks into the baby's room during naps to make sure he's breathing, the sort who imagines every latecomer in a traffic accident. I had always loved horses, though, had ridden as a teenager, and thought riding a horse might be a more fun way to lose the last fifteen pounds of pregnancy weight than riding a NordicTrack with my eyes glued to the Weather Channel, watching for tornado warnings. (I lived in Iowa then.)

The horse had been around—most recently he had lived in a field with a bunch of other horses, and before that, who knew? But he was kind and easy to ride, and most important, the second morning that I knew him, he nickered at me. That was flattering, like having a nice man call you darling but without any overtones of sexual harassment. I meant to ride three times a week; I had a baby and other children and a husband and a career. But there I was, four, five, six days a week, not just riding the horse but taking lessons, asking questions, hanging around the barn, buying equipment. I was right about the pounds—they were gone in a month—but I was wrong about everything else, namely that I was an established grown-up who had it all figured it out.

The first thing I had to confront was the same thing all adult riders have to confront—fear. Was he going to step on me? (Yes, if I didn't watch where his feet were.) Was he going to run away? (Yes, if something scared him.) Might he buck me off? (Unlikely, but possible.) More embarrassingly, was I going to fall off? (Once, yes. I was unbalanced, out of my element, weak, stiff.) Beneath the fear, I soon saw, was a long-standing habit of not actually paying attention to what I was doing. I had spent years thinking about one thing while doing another. I had, in fact, prided myself on this. But if I didn't know what I was doing and neither did the horse, he acted confused, nervous, a little scary. I had to learn, quickly but with surprising difficulty, how to pay attention.

And then there was my body. I would think *Sit up straight*, but not be able to sit up straight. I told my instructor that it didn't seem as though my head was connected to the rest of me. He agreed. (How embarrassing was that?) It was as though my nerve impulses ran through Cleveland on the way from my cerebellum to my heels. This weight-loss project was turning into a challenge of my every habit, a challenge to the unconscious way I had been living.

But the horse loved me. He nickered at me every day, came when I called, paid attention, flicking his ears when I talked. And when I did everything right, even for just a moment or two, the fear, the preoccupation, and awkwardness gave way to grace and pleasure unlike any sensation I'd ever felt, a pure physical sense of rhythm and strength that the horse communicated right into my sinews. As with all positive transformations, the right moments accumulated into right minutes and subsequently into delicious stretches of time that didn't feel like time at all.

What's unique about riding is that the horse is always right there, and not only physically: Tick Tock's personality, his intentions, and his willingness were always palpable. I learned why "out riding alone" is an oxymoron: An equestrian is never alone, is always sensing the other being, the mysterious but also understandable living being that is the horse. That is what gets me out every day, in weather I would never jog in.

My body is different now—I have triceps and biceps. I gallop and jump and ride with intense pleasure. I am also more patient, self-confident, ready for fun. I am more daring. My old "What if?" has become more of a "Why not?" I am readier to believe that if something comes up, I can deal with it—even backing up the horse trailer. But the greatest change is my constant sense of an unfolding relationship and growing knowledge. I used to pepper my trainers and vets with questions. Why is the horse doing that? What does that mean? At bottom, who is he? I discovered that the horse is life itself, a metaphor but also an example of life's mystery and unpredictability, of its generosity and beauty, a worthy object of repeated and ever-changing contemplation.

Do It Yourself

Jessica Bruder

—∗—

I am a lover of power tools. In my gas station coveralls, I've wielded welding torches, hoisted chain saws, and whiled away afternoons with a belt sander. I've mastered the plasma cutter, the nail gun, the grinder. But I believe the best tools are the ones that come standard at birth: our two hands.

Working with your hands is a big part of humanness— and, for me, happiness. A day in the woodshop or craft room or garden reconnects you with your body, which is a nice break from staring at screens. Plus, calling a plumber will not give you a sense of power and autonomy. Stopping your leaky pipe from leaking will.

Lately I've been using my hands to fix cars and grow tomatoes, unscrew lug nuts and screw together planter boxes, jack up a chassis and haul bags of dirt to the roof of my fourth-floor walk-up. I'm still a little shaky on the auto shop stuff, but I'm excited about the tomatoes, even though the hands in question don't have green thumbs. (I once killed a cactus.) No matter the results, the experience will be meaningful.

Our culture rewards expertise and efficiency. My tomatoes will reflect neither. With the cost of growing taken into account, they'll be more expensive than the ones at the supermarket. They may be less aesthetically appealing, too. But they will be mine, born of my hard work and gentle care. And that achievement, that joy, is something nobody else can create but me.

Enchanted Forest

Joyce Johnson

—∗—

I was seven or eight when my favorite aunt, Rose Wallman, who often borrowed me from my parents, came to take me for an afternoon mushrooming expedition in Forest Park, in the borough of Queens. Aunt Rose was equipped with a basket from Woolworth's and a copy of *The Little Golden Book of Mushrooms*. Forest Park was as close as you could come to a real forest in Queens. Aunt Rose, as much a neophyte mycologist as I was, delighted me by appearing to rely on my judgment in matters of life and death. We would spot a mushroom and consult *The Little Golden Book*, searching for a matching illustration. Mushroom or toadstool? (Years later, I would find myself on a blind date with a dour tax attorney, who interrupted my story at this point with a withering pronouncement: "There are no toadstools—only toxic mushrooms." "To me, at eight, they were *toadstools*," I said firmly, and shortly afterward left, alone.)

Anything Aunt Rose and I both designated "mushroom" was promptly picked. By the end of the afternoon we had gathered quite a variety; some were golden, the rest in various shades of brown. They lay nestled in Aunt Rose's basket with clinging bits of moss and pine needles. My aunt was planning to sauté the whole lot in parsley butter but said she could not take the responsibility of inviting me to share the feast. All evening I worried about her, until the phone rang. Not only had Aunt Rose survived, she reported to me that the mushrooms were delicious, and ever since I have regretted not sampling that dish, seasoned as it was with a bit of danger.

I thought of Aunt Rose often after I bought a small cabin in Vermont on the edge of the woods. She would have been pleased that I finally had my own Forest Park, complete with deer, moose, porcupines, and a bear or two. Where my lawn ends, there are wild apple trees and blackberry brambles. In the fall after it rains, I'm likely to find boletes in the garden. My friends and neighbors up there are experienced mushroom hunters who wisely collect only what they're absolutely sure of and eat everything they gather. Strings of dried mushrooms hang from the rafters of their kitchens. If you're out driving with them, they're likely to stop the car to harvest giant speckled pheasant's backs jutting from dead elms along the roadside or the slightly phosphorescent shaggy manes that show up at night, luminous in the headlights. I've heard tales of giant puffballs, big enough to serve six, and of certain outcroppings of morels in hillside cow pastures. If you ask, "But where exactly do you find your morels?" you won't get an answer—such secrets are respected by all—but you will get an invitation to come to dinner and try some.

I bought an enormous illustrated tome on mushrooms, full of Latin names and stern warnings and symbols representing degrees of edibility. I studied the picture of the lovely white mushroom known as the angel of death, learned how to make spore prints on paper towels, and felt properly nervous but still eager to proceed. Finally I went off to the woods without my mushroom bible, which was far too heavy to carry. I was a middle-aged city dweller still unaccustomed to being alone in the woods, and sometimes I thought I had to be crazy as I scrambled down the ravines and over fallen tree trunks and wrenched my sneakers out of oozing mud. If I broke my leg, who would find me?

Perhaps days would pass before my friends worried. After my rescue they'd ask, "What were you thinking?!" The truth would be somewhat ridiculous: "I wanted chanterelles."

I'd been told they grew everywhere in Vermont, and even for a beginner like me, the delicious little saffron trumpets were easily identifiable. I found only three or four that first day, growing out of rotted logs, but still it was a victory. I put them in an omelet. I liked the way the urge to seek them cleared out my mind, brought purpose and suspense to my rambles; I thought of nothing in the woods but of spotting a few dots of cadmium yellow. One day, wandering contentedly in circles, I lost my way. I headed toward the sunlight and found myself in a strangely familiar place that turned out to be my neighbor's yard. There was a lone chanterelle growing in his driveway. With a twinge of guilt, I picked it.

My city cat had come to Vermont with me; I'd kept her in the house but finally she made her escape through some torn screening. I ran after her, tearfully calling her name, but she melted into the woods. As I walked back to the house, I found myself in a stand of birches near the road, only a few yards from my door. The ground was covered with small yellow trumpets, more than I'd ever hoped to see in one spot. They'd been hiding in plain sight—like the cat, as it turned out. She materialized on the porch at five the next morning, ravenously hungry and full of fleas.

So thanks to her I have my own secret place. I can only guess at what makes the chanterelles so abundant there. Is it the particular amount of sunlight filtering through the trees, the birch bark and decaying limbs on the ground mixed with just the right proportions of maple leaves and pine needles? My chanterelles keep coming back year after year, and I gather them, reveling in the mystery of their bounty.

Varied Treasure

Lisa Congdon

—✳—

Years ago my partner and I were walking past a garage sale in San Francisco when I spotted a piece of midcentury Norwegian enamelware—a bowl in a blue lotus pattern. It's really rare, a great find. The asking price? One dollar.

The bowl was worth about $150—but it's not about the money. I loved knowing I was the only person around who understood its value. I've always loved that. When I was a girl in upstate New York, I made my grandmother take me to the dump to look for treasure; she was a collector too. When I was told to clean my room, I would instead arrange my collections—arranging was always my favorite part. There's something so appealing about an array of like things—so orderly and pretty.

My advice is to find something special to you and start seeking it out. It doesn't matter if it's worth money; it just needs to be something you want more than one of. And it should be hard to find, because the hunt is half the fun. I like collecting the way I like crime novels: I want to awaken my inner detective. The longer the search, the sweeter the find.

Horizons: Expanded

Heather Greenwood Davis

—✳—

We arrive in Chengdu on a pitch-black morning on the overnight train from Xi'an. As my husband, Ish, our two young sons, Ethan and Cameron, and I stumble groggily out of the station, we sidestep poorer travelers huddled on flattened boxes on the freezing concrete. China's eleventh largest city, home to a famous panda research facility, feels lonely and uninviting. It doesn't help that we've forgotten to have our hotel's name written down for us in Chinese, and the taxi drivers swarming us don't speak English. They pull at my sons, who are clutching my waist. Suddenly a man carrying a laptop approaches. "Where are you trying to go?" he asks. Soon he's negotiating with a driver, and not long after that we're laughing with him over breakfast at our hotel. He turns out to be a visiting professor from Singapore. "I couldn't just leave you out there to fend for yourselves," he tells us. As we're cooing over pictures of his baby daughter, I lock eyes with Ish across the table: We know this never would have happened back in Toronto.

In 2011, when Ish was offered a sabbatical from his job as a public health inspector, we set out to see the world for a year with our kids (as a journalist, my job has always been flexible). We aren't rich or crazy; we just saw an opportunity to live our dreams and seized it, selling our car, renting out our house, and exhausting our savings. Over the next twelve months we visited twenty-nine countries, soaring in a hot-air balloon above King Tut's tomb, riding ostriches in Vietnam, and scrubbing four-ton elephants in Thailand.

But the moments we'll remember most involve people, not places. When we joined in a moonlit game of Ping-Pong in a Cairo alleyway with our city guide's neighbors, for example, or dined on duck confit in the minimalist home of a worldly Parisian family for whom we'd snapped a photo in Seville, or sat cross-legged on the floor of the one-room home of a Cambodian tuk-tuk driver who wanted his kids to meet ours. We'd expected to be four alone in the world, but in these moments—when we relied on instinct and trusted strangers—we became a part of it. I'd always taught my children to be wary of anyone they didn't know, but in Buenos Aires I watched with pride as my shy seven-year-old gathered his courage and marched into a soccer game some local kids were playing. In the Galápagos Islands, I beamed when my picky nine-year-old tasted—and loved—lobster tail on the advice of some new friends in our tour group. As for Ish and me, we learned that people are kinder than we'd given them credit for. We stopped seeing the planet as a list of places to visit and started daydreaming about whom, exactly, we'd meet next.

Back home in Canada, we now chat with the grocery clerk whose Portuguese accent we can place and share a joke with the taxi driver whose rearview-mirror flag we recognize. We linger to make a friend, where once we might have rushed by. And we get a glorious connection, a world-size dose of happiness, in return.

The Joy of Discovery

✳

I believe that if you'll just stand up and go,
life will open up for you.

—TINA TURNER

Burning Questions

Katie Arnold-Ratliff

—✳—

Remember when you were little and you felt you might explode because you had so many questions? (Why is the sky blue? Why are zebras striped? How come I can't have another Popsicle?) And remember how good that felt—to find the world so fascinating that you had to learn, this second and in great detail, exactly how it worked?

How did we lose touch with that desire to ask, ask, ask? Was it when we became busy, distracted, overwhelmed grown-ups, feigning expertise, acting like we know everything all the time?

Know everything? Were we even listening in Intro to Philosophy? Did we miss the part where Socrates, who supposedly said, "I know that I know nothing," developed an entire method of figuring out stuff based entirely on *inquiry?* And that all knowledge exists precisely because people have, persistently and for centuries, asked tons and tons of questions?

Have we established that questions are marvelous, momentous things? And if so, can we agree that asking ourselves the right ones can have life-altering effects? Because have you ever noticed how questions prevent us from settling for less than we deserve? That asking ourselves *Could it be better?* is a great way to make things, well, a whole lot better? That a bunch of our breakthroughs, triumphs, and joys occurred when we asked a few big, bold, paradigm-shifting questions? Don't we owe it to ourselves—don't we deserve—to live an examined life? Can it be said that asking questions is what keeps us honest, drives us to aim higher—and is the very thing that makes us human?

In a word? Yes. No question about it.

The Eye of the Beholder

Sister Wendy Beckett

—✳—

How can I describe what happened when I encountered for the first time the spiritual power of great furniture? In all my visits to museums, I have usually walked past furniture on my eager way to "the real thing": paintings, sculptures, and ceramics. But in the Boston Museum of Fine Arts some years ago, I had the good fortune to meet Jonathan, a curator of American decorative arts and sculpture, and my eyes were opened. I saw, as he did, how furniture can have a majestic sculptural beauty that can stop one in one's tracks. One such work was the *Cogswell Boston Bombé Chest-on-Chest* of 1782. It swells in a stately curve up to a surge of mahogany drawers and climaxes in an insouciant pediment, crowned with the American eagle. (This was early Boston, remember.) I was looking at glorious works of art—furniture, indeed, but even more, they were pieces shaped and crafted by a master hand. Beauty came at me from all dimensions, from unexpected angles, offering an enlargement of spirit I still cannot wholly comprehend.

What If the Hokey Pokey Really *Is* What It's All About?

Sue Fliess

—✳—

While heading to the grocery store one morning, I stopped at a light behind an old Chevy sorely in need of a paint job. A teenager was driving, blaring music with the windows down. Her bumper was scuffed. One taillight was crushed. But she didn't seem to mind. Her manicured fingers tapped the steering wheel like red-tipped drumsticks, her hair lifting in the breeze. She sang at the top of her voice, ignoring the audience around her. I liked her.

Just before the light changed and she drove off, I noticed her car had a bumper sticker: WHAT IF THE HOKEY POKEY REALLY *IS* WHAT IT'S ALL ABOUT?

Then I thought, *Wait, what if it is?*

It could have been my mood that day, or it could have

been destiny. But idling behind that Chevy, all at once it occurred to me that I'd left no room in my life for simple delight. I scheduled, penciled in, or planned everything from my kids' playdates to dinner with friends months in advance, just to get it off my mind—which, more and more, was swamped with a nonstop, fire-hose-like onslaught of obligations. Where were the moments when I could rap on the steering wheel with my hair blowing in the wind?

So now I'm trying to make time to enjoy the sweet, simple, inconsequential bits of life, wherever and however I can. We just celebrated my son's eleventh birthday at a laser tag arena. If you've never set foot in one, it's loud, crowded, and smells like feet; the old me would have gladly opted out, waiting in the birthday party room, setting up the pizza and cake, checking e-mail. The new me got suited up, chose a laser tag handle (Mominator), and ventured in alongside a dozen of my son's friends with vest, laser gun, and survival instincts in tow. It was awesome—I didn't even come in last.

It also turns out that when I'm not obsessing over getting things done, getting to the next destination, getting my point across, and moving right along, I hear a lot more. Yesterday my nine-year-old wanted to tell me his side of an argument he'd had with his brother. "Please, Mom," he said, "just listen before you say anything." So I did as he asked. I listened, and had a revelation: The outcome of the altercation didn't matter to him as much as being heard by me did. I chose to be in that moment with him for as long as it lasted. I want more encounters like that. I'm starting—one foot at a time—to put my whole self in.

My Own Best Friend

Robin Romm

—✳—

In my early thirties, I moved from a small bungalow in the Bay Area to a hippie barn in Santa Fe to take a new job. The barn, with its tin doors and weathered wood, had seemed novel, a radical change. Here my boyfriend and I would explore our mellow sides, walking the dog on dusty horse trails, eating dinner at our picnic table. It sounded romantic.

But soon after we unpacked, he left for a monthlong writing fellowship in another state. I found myself in this new, rural place alone. And I panicked. Though I'd grown up an only child, I no longer knew how to sit with myself for long stretches of time. And honestly, my childhood had been lonely. My parents both had busy, demanding careers and a penchant for budget babysitters who did little more than watch television and talk on the phone. I spent great swaths of time inventing games by myself in my room. As soon as I was old enough to drive, I hung out constantly with friends, a habit that persisted throughout my twenties. I wasn't all that interested in reclaiming solitude. During the first week alone in the barn, I called every person in my phone, even people I barely knew. But after I'd talked to everyone, after my eyes nearly fell out of my head from watching TV, I realized I couldn't keep this up for four weeks.

So I did something I'd always wanted to do: I signed up for banjo lessons.

At night I practiced, looking out at the sunsets over the chamisa flowers, the jackrabbits loping by. When I got tired of the chord progressions, I'd knit or read. And though I expected to be dogged by loneliness—that mortal childhood enemy—I felt, instead, a surprising calm. All this time, I'd been working so hard to avoid myself, but as it turned out, I liked being alone. Me and myself had so many shared interests, so much to say to each other! If I permitted it, I was good company. That felt like such a revelation.

The longest relationship we have with anyone is with

ourselves, and yet that relationship is often the first one we let slide. Maintaining it brings such comfort, though: Liking your company means that you always have at your beck and call a person who gets you.

So, if everyone departs and you're left feeling lonely and adrift—or if you never allow yourself to be alone—ask yourself what you'd do if you had a friend over. You'd be curious about her, you'd engage with her, you'd be compassionate. Why not treat yourself the same way?

Seeing in the Dark

Thelma Adams

—✳—

During the New York City blackout of 2003, on the 8.2-mile walk from my midtown Manhattan office to my Brooklyn brownstone (a trek that included two Mister Softee ice-cream stops and the crossing of one immense bridge), I had four unmapped hours to take stock of where I stood at forty-four and spontaneously consider how my life needed changing.

When I was in my twenties and single, I'd had similar moments in airplanes flying coast to coast. On either end of the journey, life flowed in all its chaos and complexity, its conflicting desires and demands. But airborne, in the pause between departure and destination, strapped in beside strangers, I often found myself contemplating my life as a whole and reaching big decisions about it.

After the lights went out in New York, as I headed south in velvet slippers I'd bought months earlier in Chinatown, my high heels tucked into a bag slung over my shoulder, I walked the same streets I'd come to, as a young woman, from California. I passed the Strand bookstore, the Little Italy apartment where a friend had shared a bathroom wall with the gangster John Gotti, the bar where my husband, Ranald, and I practically floated the brilliant autumn day that we declared our love for each other.

That sweltering August afternoon, people crammed the sidewalks in moods that ranged from joy to apocalyptic panic. Among the frazzled, the communal worry was that this was not simply a power outage but a repeat of the terrorist attacks of 9/11—the beginning of the end, again.

For me, something snapped that day, although I didn't hear it for all the noise in the street. Darkness fell while I crossed the Brooklyn Bridge; I was tired, and the soles of my slippers were wearing thin. I wondered if I would make it home, if my family was all right, if the surprising peace of the afternoon would be preserved until I crossed my threshold.

Nearly twenty years had passed since I first came to the city. I was the mother of two small children. When I wasn't working—writing a (still unpublished) novel and reviewing movies—I walked the streets with an overpacked stroller, dreading the subways for their steep, stroller-hostile stairs. And Ranald, who had moved to New York for me, had debilitating asthma, which had worsened to the point where he was allergic to the city itself: the mold in the subway, the cockroaches in the basement, the dust.

A year later, inspired by what I saw in my heart on that long walk, on that dark night, I changed direction: We moved to a hunting lodge on 14.5 acres in upstate New York. And if I had misgivings at leaving behind hard-won friends and perfect pizza slices, they vanished in the wonder that is country life.

In the country, blackouts are a more common, less public occurrence. A tree falls. Lightning strikes. A stream floods its banks. The computer crashes midsentence. The washer halts midcycle. The electric lights dim and then go out entirely. We leave the refrigerator-freezer doors shut in hopes that the power outage won't last too long and we can keep that terrific lamb curry Ranald made.

For the last hours of daylight, we hang on cheerfully, reading in corners by the windows, sweeping the kitchen floor, bundling the newspapers. But as twilight falls, and we migrate toward the screened porch and the last shreds of light, and the color begins to wash from the brilliant goldfinches at their feeder, Ranald curses the fact that we didn't buy a generator. Eleven-year-old Trevor experiences computer withdrawal.

We draw around the stubby white candles bought in bulk for just such an occasion, and though I'm well aware of my son's aversion to performing, I suggest the impossible: Why doesn't Trevor get out his guitar and show me what he can do after a year of lessons? He drags out the left-handed instrument I haven't heard him play since the lessons began. He runs through his repertoire—the chords G, C, E, and his favorite: G7. We get a bit of melody, a random made-up tune. His even features are serious and keen and focused over the frets and strings, and I see why guitarists make girls fall in love.

After Trevor plays his song, he picks up the flashlight, making wide, abstract arcs like ribbons against the blackness. Lizzy begins to dance, stomping her heels on the cement. Trevor flashes the light on his little sister, around her, above her, so that her shadow falls on the scrim of the screen. Outside, a bullfrog croaks; the finches prattle at the feeder. The kids are still playing together, tied by the ribbon of light, when we notice a revived glow deep within the forgotten house. Ranald goes to check the temps in the fridge-freezer, Lizzy turns on the TV, Trevor reboots his computer, and I head to my office to check e-mail. We scatter in the light, but in my head I can still feel the rhythms of my son's newfound chords, my daughter's shadowy flamenco.

There is no big decision to be made now. My life doesn't need changing. But it is extraordinary to realize that this infinitely happy moment, framed in time—not the memories, not the expectations or ambitions—is my life. And in this moment I change tense: I stop becoming and just am.

The Lesson

Hilene Flanzbaum

—✳—

I am not an optimist. I don't believe that the glass is half full. I am the granddaughter of four Eastern European Jews who fled Poland to escape pogroms. When it is sunny, I look for rain. When the phone rings after ten P.M., I start planning the funeral. My favorite joke is: "Jewish telegram— 'Start worrying; details to follow.'" I tell you this so you will not think of me as a perky, upbeat person, in denial of every dark emotion she has ever had. Nor am I religious, or even sure I believe in God. I am dark; my hair is dark; my eyes are dark. And so, as both an intellectual and a cynic, I have trouble admitting this but here goes: Having breast cancer changed my life—for the better.

Lots of survivors say something like this. I have

even heard some say, "Breast cancer was the best thing that ever happened to me." I had always viewed this remark with skepticism—"Boy, that must be one great antidepressant. . . ."

I had the bad mammogram on March 13, 2001, the first day of spring break. I was forty-two years old and had two daughters, six and eight. The year before, the technician had taken one picture, come back and said simply, "You can go home." "I can?" I asked. I had expected worse. In 2001, I got it. The technician took the first picture and came back for another. And another. And then they made me wait for a sonogram. Then they made me wait to talk to the radiologist. He was unsympathetic—grouchy even—and unmovable. "You are going to want to have this looked at," he said. He didn't say, "It's probably nothing, but . . ." That's what all my girlfriends had heard. But he wouldn't say that. Instead, when I pushed him for any comforting words, he said gruffly, "Well, if it's cancer, we've gotten it early."

I have nothing cheerful to say about the next three and a half months. It was all horrible—the waiting was the worst. After that initial mammogram, I waited three weeks for a biopsy. I knew it was cancer. "But your mother never had breast cancer," friends said. I knew I had cancer. Just as

I'd known I would not "just lose" the forty pounds I gained during my first pregnancy. "Oh, it just slips off," women said. "Slips off?" I thought. "On me, it is not going to slip off." And I was right. My mother's friends said, "Oh, she'll have a lumpectomy and radiation and be done with it." I didn't believe that either, and I was right. After two attempts to get clean margins, I had a mastectomy on the right side; the following year when the tech found precancerous cells on the left side, I had one on that side.

So after having a double mastectomy by the time I was forty-three, where is the bright side?

First I noticed that I was noticing my life. It was as if someone had stood next to me in the supermarket line and yelled in my ear, in the loudest voice imaginable—"Wake up!!!!" I stopped sleepwalking through my days. I started paying attention. I won't say clichéd things like "colors seemed brighter" or "flowers smelled sweeter." I am not sure they did. I just felt a new sense grow in me—I became conscious of time; I was alert in a new way.

Second benefit: I realized I'd spent too much time in my life doing things I didn't want to do. When my in-laws wanted the family to fly across the country to celebrate Thanksgiving, I actually said to my husband, "No, I am tired and I don't want to spend my vacation traveling. I am not doing that." I joined a highly compensated committee where a belligerent and simpleminded colleague bullied me—and, get this, I quit. Just like that. "I don't care about the money. I am not going back," I said to my husband. And I didn't.

Third: My husband and I stopped quarreling. Why did we ever bother? What could have been that important? My relationship with my sister got better. Half a lifetime of sibling rivalry evaporated like smoke.

Most important, having breast cancer focused me on my children like a laser. I was always an attentive mother, but a working one, and a conflicted one. The feeling that I should always be in the other place trailed me like a whining dog. Now I want to spend every minute humanly possible with my children. They are far and away more important to me than anything on earth. I want to spend time looking at their faces, building their strength and courage. And since cancer, I have, without the slightest twinge.

Finally, and best of all, I have stopped expecting the worst. Worrying should prepare you for disaster, but it doesn't. I learned that nothing prepares you. We spend so much time in our lives suffering, we don't need any dress rehearsals. The worst will find us, and you know what? We will have to deal with it when it does.

My life is better now; more heartily felt. Last year I returned to writing poetry—all the poems are about the possibility of finding joy. This past soccer season, I met my breast surgeon at the field where his children play alongside mine. We embraced like survivors of a catastrophe who meet again after a long while. "Who was that?" my daughter asked afterward. "You really like him." "Yes," I replied, "I do really like him. He was my doctor when I was sick; he is a wonderful, wonderful man, and I am better for having known him." Would I have chosen a life where I did not get to meet him? Yes. Would I have been happier in that life? No, I don't think so.

Awed and Amazed

You must habit yourself to the dazzle of the light
and of every moment of your life.

—WALT WHITMAN

Walking with Devotion

Mary Oliver

—✳—

When I walk out into the world, I take no thoughts with me. That's not easy, but you can learn to do it. An empty mind is hungry, so you look at everything longer, and closer. Don't hum! When you listen with empty ears, you hear more. And this is the core of the secret: Attention is the beginning of devotion.

Graced by Her Present

Meghan O'Rourke

—✳—

Like many people, I want serenity in my day-to-day life, yet I'm obsessive enough about the smallest details that a moment of calm is hard to find. In my twenties, I worked as if focus could be some kind of salvation, endlessly worrying about my next project and missing family gatherings and forgetting to buy Christmas presents in the process. Once, when I managed to make it home for a visit, my mother, who had her bird-watching books out, put her hand on my arm and said, "I don't want you just to go from hill to hill, Meg. You should stop to enjoy the view."

After my mother died, at the age of fifty-five, I thought a lot about what she'd said, and I came to realize she'd given me an important gift: her presence. As my father put it one night when we were talking, "Your mother just had a way of being there, and it made everything better." Listening to him, I knew I wanted more of that "way of being there" in my own life.

Losing my mother—as painful as it was—has brought with it a blessing I could not have anticipated. It has led me to realign my sense of focus, my values, my attention. "Lighten up, Meg," my mother liked to say when she saw how easily I became blindsided by anxiety. Now I try to honor her example by learning to relax into the daily chaos, by keeping in mind the majestic strangeness of the world, and the smallness of my place in it.

Being present is easier said than done, of course. Presence requires letting go of old habits, complaints, and hang-ups. In my case, it also required recognizing my competitiveness and impatience; I had to step back to notice the ways I am hard on people, judging them when I should just support them, insisting things be done on my punishing schedule. Today I make more time to sit and listen when a friend is troubled by something. I climb fewer hills.

My mother was a great gift giver, at once thoughtful and sly (one year she put little bottles of energy drinks in my stocking). But her greatest gift remains the way she approached life; she didn't let anything frazzle her to the point where she didn't have time to listen and laugh with us. Sometimes I picture her face and feel the sting of loss, but then sorrow blossoms into the happiness of knowing how much she gave me. A joy spreads like sunlight, and it's as if I can hear her saying, "Lighten up, Meg." Finally, I know what she meant.

Everyday Magic

Kathryn Sullivan

—*—

I used to live a few hundred yards outside the Johnson Space Center in Houston. Early each morning, I'd drive about three minutes to the center—that was my commute. On October 14, 1984, I was technically off for the day, since I'd just landed from my first space flight the night before. But I wanted to see all our photos. I'd had this great experience—one I'd dreamed of forever and worked toward for ages—and it had lasted only seven days. I kept looking at the sky, still wishing I was up *there*.

On my drive in that morning, though, I noticed a bunch of migrating birds flying in various V shapes, forming and re-forming as they do, crossing in front of the last bit of sunrise color in the sky. *Now that's a good reason to be back*, I thought, surprising myself. Sunrise and birds—nothing out of the ordinary, but not something you can see in space. Suddenly it was nice to be on Earth again.

An Extraordinary Machine

Lila Keary

—✳—

I swim lean, vigorous strokes through an alexandrite blue ocean. I laugh and dive and let the sun wash over my face. I sprint and swoop and ride the waves. And then I wake up.

My bedroom develops like a Polaroid, getting sharper as it comes slowly into focus. There on the night table are nine different pills and a syringe I've set out for the morning. Beside them are the sterile gauze and Betadine I use to clean the catheter that's sewn into my chest. The bottle of Betadine not only disinfects, it also serves as a paperweight for the dozen insurance forms that need to be filled out and mailed before the weekend. On the other side of my bed hangs an IV drip for nutrition and hydration.

doesn't kill me sure does keep me from riding many waves.

I've had cancer for a third of my life. I've watched people get well and I've watched people die while I scramble from standard drug to new procedure to experimental protocol, buying time till the next big breakthrough. These treatments chip at my body bit by bit. They've screwed up both my kidneys and damaged my heart. They've made the soles of my feet burn and my fingertips numb. There's no vision in my left eye; my digestive system is shot; I've become severely prone to depression, unable to have a baby or a frozen margarita or any long-term plans. What's that old joke about the ad for a lost dog? "Blind, incontinent, no teeth, missing right leg, tail, and part of an ear. Answers to the name Lucky."

I'd love to say that you've caught me at an off moment, but the fact is I whine a lot. (A fellow patient once told me he'd never heard anyone complain so much—and he'd spent nineteen months in the Hanoi Hilton.) It seems one of the unspoken side effects of cancer (at least for me) is extreme crankiness. My body has betrayed me and I'm mad as hell. But wallowing in righteous indignation only gets a girl so far. So these days I'm focusing on what this decidedly soft, slightly used, utterly ridiculous forty-one-year-old body *can* do.

And what I can do is make the best kid I know laugh hysterically simply by feigning shock and revulsion at the sight of a plastic tarantula. I can pitch a baseball, though word on the street is that I throw like a girl—or worse, like Chuck Knoblauch. I can cook a chicken Marbella that makes people from Marbella (okay, Brooklyn) beg for the recipe. Furthermore, I have what can only be described as a superhuman gift for picking ripe pineapples. I can listen closely to my friends, my instincts, and Glenn Gould playing the "Goldberg Variations"—which I'm told Bach wrote for a Russian count with severe insomnia. On my better days, I can do laundry, dishes, and all things sexual. I can hold down a full-time job, hold up my end of the conversation, and shop with the kind of frenzied abandon seldom seen outside of Times Square on New Year's Eve.

Control isn't always possible, but feeling and imagination and a touch of transcendence are. I've taken to grabbing a cup of tea and heading for the roof of my Lower East Side apartment building on mornings when sleep doesn't seem to be an option. Last Thursday at 6:40 A.M., it was pouring. The drops of rain pelting against tin flowerpots sounded like bacon frying. The air smelled like geraniums and lasagna—the old Italian restaurant on the ground floor was already prepping for the lunch crowd. My sweatpants were soaked, my hair was dripping, one of my slippers was floating away, but lights were starting to switch on all over the neighborhood. Oyster-colored trench coats and black umbrellas were beginning to make their way down Second Avenue. Here were people and puddles and pigeons and trees and taxis, and I got to experience every deliciously drenched inch of it.

I have cancer but I also have windy summer mornings in the rain and an active sense of awe at all that I can still touch and taste and see and hear and breathe in at any given moment. I have the crystal-clear understanding that recovery is worth only as much as the life you recover.

The Big Picture

Neil deGrasse Tyson

—✳—

Throughout their lives, stars turn basic elements like hydrogen and helium into richer, heavier elements. When they die, some stars then scatter their remains, full of those enriched ingredients, into gas clouds across the galaxy, where they'll later regroup and become part of a brand-new star system. It's poetic—the next generation of stars benefiting from those that came before. To me, that's a powerful message: Instead of worrying about getting older and whether we're as athletic or pretty or thin as we used to be, we can focus on leading a brilliant life that will be remembered. Make an impact; even if your job doesn't help save lives, you can create art or do something that will bring joy to someone else. You should celebrate each day that you're able to leave a lasting effect. It means that even as you get older, the universe will someday be a little bit better because you've lived in it.

Oh, What a Thrill!

✳

All I can say about life is, Oh God, enjoy it!

—BOB NEWHART

The Cheering Section

Valerie Monroe

—*—

I had accompanied my four-year-old son in a crowd of similar couples to a showing of *Peter Pan*. We were a rowdy group—lots of running and screaming in the aisles, seat jumping, and general expectant, disorganized glee. But once the movie began, we quickly settled into a quieter mode; many of the kids—my son among them—climbed comfortably into their parents' laps.

So there we all were, cozy, rapt, when Tinker Bell's light started to go out, and Peter turned toward us with his plea to save her: "Clap! Clap if you believe in fairies!" Instantly, my son and all the other children began to clap—what sweet innocence!—at first in a light, helpful patter, but as Tink's light flickered and grew, they clapped with increasing enthusiasm, and at Peter's exhortations, they clapped heartily with great, serious determination. Very soon we moms and dads were clapping too, and many of us also stamping our feet and whistling till, when Tink regained her radiant spark, the whole place exploded in a triumphant, earsplitting crescendo of unanimous rejoicing.

And I wept. An ordinary Saturday afternoon, a theater full of antsy kids, a story I'd heard a thousand times—who would have thought there would be opportunity for such surrender and celebration? But I shouldn't have been surprised. For the longest time, I have been falling face-first into it everywhere: puddles of awe, as I notice the intricate patterns of rain blown against my window; rivers of it, as I paddle in a kayak beside the city and turn to see a range of towering skyscrapers, peaks of sparkling glass, majestic in the brilliant autumn sun. Maybe you have these moments too—commonplace in every way except for your active appreciation—when engagement floods your senses, drenching you in pleasure, when there's no past to regret or future to worry over, just the shining, magnificent, awe-inspiring now.

Naked and Laughing

Amy Bloom

—✳—

The first time I really thought about nakedness, about my own naked body in particular, about the fact that animals were always naked and people almost never were, I was in my neighbor's swimming pool. I was around eight and the older kids had gone to get snacks and towels. The adults were doing adult things. I was the only person in a fifty-foot-long blue basin filled with eighty-degree water. I slipped off my shoulder straps and suddenly rolled down my suit, caught it with my toe and flipped it onto the cement edge of the pool. I did the breaststroke for one lap and my own myopic, lifted-head crawl for another. For however long it takes three kids to make bologna sandwiches and find beach towels, I was in a new world, like the first man on the moon, had Neil Armstrong been given to giggling.

No one had mentioned this world to me. I went from pajamas to underwear to clothes every morning and back the other way every night. And somehow no one had said anything to me about what a good time was to be had between pajamas and underwear. After my Saturday of Nakedness, you might think there'd have been no stopping me. There was *plenty* stopping me: my parents, both of whom appeared, even in my dreams, fully clothed; school; boys; cold weather. But when I could, I'd lie under our willow tree, shielded by its long green curtain, and read P. G. Wodehouse and Dorothy Parker in nothing but my socks. Naked and laughing.

Best Naked Saturday Since I Was Eight: The man I love is standing in front of me, in our bedroom. He's not naked; he's actually more than naked: He's wearing an undershirt, a very wide, white, and necessary mesh-and-Velcro lumbar support wrap, and the navy blue socks that are usually hidden by his suit trousers. His boxers are off because he's coming to bed; his undershirt and socks are on because his terrible back pain makes both the reaching up and the bending over difficult. He looks at himself in the mirror and laughs out loud. He puts his black fedora on his head and models the whole look for me.

Naked and laughing. Can't beat it.

My Unplanned Adventure

Catherine Price

—✳—

It was Friday night in Shinjuku, a Tokyo neighborhood famous for neon signs, subterranean shopping malls, and rent-by-the-hour lodgings known as love hotels. In crowded bars, people tipped back beers and sang karaoke. Young men with black jackets and gelled hair stood on street corners, offering menus of available escorts to passersby. In the midst of the action was a store window, covered except for a narrow strip of glass. If you were to have stopped and looked through it, you would have seen something strange: my legs, submerged to the ankles, with six-hundred flesh-eating fish feasting on my feet.

This is the story of how I got there.

Like many people, I approach vacations with a level

of preparation appropriate for a medical licensing exam—poring over Internet reviews, reading guidebooks cover to cover, and studying maps so I'm oriented from the moment my plane touches down. I research, I plan, I strategize, transforming my trips into long to-do lists I must conquer in order for them to be judged a success.

This tendency was in full effect during a recent week my husband and I spent on Kauai, when I broke the island into quadrants and made long lists of every activity we should do while "relaxing" in paradise. It was exhausting and, somewhere in the process, I started to ask myself why I was doing this. What was I trying to accomplish? What if, instead of meticulously planning, I were to just show up in a new place and let the experience unfold? By stage-managing every detail, I realized, I was ruining one of the best parts of travel: the adventure.

So I decided to take a different approach. I would go on a trip in which I relinquished control. No guidebook, no Internet research, no list of things to see or do. Instead, I would base all my activities, from where I stayed to what I ate or saw, on the recommendations of strangers. Even the destination would be chosen by someone else.

I started by approaching a woman in the fiction section of a San Francisco bookstore and asking her to tell me the most interesting place she'd ever been. She responded, "I love Tokyo," and two weeks later, I boarded a flight. I had a map. That was it.

The ambition of this project didn't fully sink in until the plane took off and I realized I was going to have to ask a stranger where to bunk. At first that made me nervous—aren't strangers the same people who steal wallets and kidnap children? But then I looked at the passengers around me. A woman in the next row wore a bumblebee neck pillow. The girl in the seat next to me had adorned each long, fake fingernail with a plastic Hello Kitty charm, as if worried a customs agent might demand a finger puppet show. These, I realized, were not the strangers my mother had warned me about.

I asked a flight attendant to recommend a hotel for the night, and he consulted the rest of the Tokyo-based crew. Several minutes later, he found me in the darkened cabin and handed me a piece of paper with suggestions, including "Asakusa."

"This is my neighborhood," he said, introducing himself as Yori. "And this," he pointed at a different word, "is a hostel popular with backpackers." I hadn't even arrived in Tokyo and I had already learned two important lessons. First, it's not that scary to ask people for help. Second, I should dress better.

One hypothesis for why we love guidebooks so much is that relying on experts alleviates our fear of the unknown and makes us feel more in control. It's an approach that makes total sense, except for one thing: It's an ineffective way to plan a fun trip.

The problem with guidebooks has to do with what psychologists call affective forecasting—our ability to predict our emotional (that is, "affective") reaction to a future event. It's a skill at which we're not particularly good. We overestimate how much a positive event will improve our lives; we underestimate our ability to bounce back from hardship. And when it comes to travel, we're likely to be remarkably bad at predicting how much we'll enjoy the very experiences we've so carefully planned.

Instead of basing our decisions on our own analysis, we should just ask other people whether they had a good time. There's ample research to back this up, but I still fall into the large camp of people who find it hard to believe that strangers could be better than a guidebook at predicting what I'll like.

So I was surprised when I emerged from the train

station at Asakusa. The northeast Tokyo neighborhood would never have jumped out at me on a map, but it was perfect. Instead of the high-rises and endless brand-name stores that characterize downtown, Asakusa was filled with charismatic pedestrian streets lined with small shops and restaurants, and was home to the Sensō-ji temple, the oldest in Tokyo. After dropping my bags at the hostel—which was clean, if basic—I asked for a restaurant recommendation in English from a young mother on the street and ended up in a small restaurant that specialized in tempura. Soon I was digging into the waitress's favorite dish: a bowl of fried shrimp on top of rice. It wasn't the best tempura I'd ever had, but I didn't care. Alone in a strange city on my first night in town, I felt inspired by my experiences thus far—and excited about what might happen next.

Before collapsing in the hostel, I asked a woman who had helped me find a towel what I should do if I woke up early, a likely scenario, since 2:00 A.M. in Tokyo was 9:00 A.M. the day before on America's West Coast. She suggested the Tsukiji Market. This wasn't particularly creative—Tsukiji is one of the biggest tourist attractions in the city, as well known as the Empire State Building or Times Square. But at 4:00 in the morning, what else was I going to do?

When I awoke at 3:30, sans alarm clock, I was tempted to stay in bed on principle—but I fought the urge and headed into the dark. The streets were deserted, the subway uncharacteristically empty, and I was surprised when I walked out of the station into a stream of people sweeping me toward the cavernous market.

Tsukiji operated at the speed of a stock exchange. Motorized carts barreled down its wet streets in unpredictable directions, forklifts hoisted pallets of sea creatures onto trucks, and no matter where I stood, I was in someone's way. Worried about meeting my doom under a box of soft-shelled crabs, I stuck close to a row of parked trucks and soon entered the main area of the market. Rows of stalls displayed Styrofoam containers of fresh seafood—eels, mackerel, tightly coiled tentacles of octopus—each booth presided over by vendors wearing overcoats to keep out the cold.

The sun had barely begun to rise, but at the back of the market, the daily fish auction was already under way. Dozens of enormous frozen tuna lay on the ground in a large warehouse, each with a round steak cut from its tail and attached to its body by a piece of colored plastic rope. Buyers in black galoshes moved methodically from tuna to tuna, jabbing the exposed flesh of the tail with ook-tipped wooden sticks to determine the fattiness of the meat. As I watched, a man climbed atop a small box and began frantically ringing a small bell. Then, in a torrent of Japanese and hand signals, he auctioned off the fish. Despite the other tourists packed around me, I felt exhilarated, as if I'd stumbled onto something secret.

I should pause here to explain my method of communication. Figuring that most people's English would be as nonexistent as my Japanese, I'd had a fluent friend translate an introduction and several key questions, which I'd printed out on oversize cards and now carried in my bag. If I wanted to ask people their favorite dish or sight to see, I would show them the card, have them write down the answer, and have someone else tell me what it said. (It was an excellent system overall, but beware Google Translate. Based on its software, my introductory card read: "Put fear! My name is Kasharin Price . . . . We are forced to travel to ask your opinion of the residents there, since the threshold and what to look funny or what should I do.")

Other than seeking variety, I had no criteria for the people I approached—the first person who made eye contact with me usually got a card. Such was the case with a woman selling greens in a produce market next to Tsukiji. One smile tossed my way, and I thrust a question into her hands. It read, "What is your favorite restaurant?" so I tried to explain, via hand gestures, that what I *actually* meant was "I am hungry for breakfast but already had a large bowl of shrimp tempura for dinner, so could you recommend something a little lighter?" She shook her head shyly and handed it back.

A few days later, a stranger recommended a restaurant called AMOR. When I arrived I sat at the bar, which was decorated with a model train set left over from the previous owner. With one station in Asakusa and the other in a German Alpine village, the train was an odd addition to a French-Spanish restaurant in Tokyo. But the food lived up to the boundary-bending vibe: I tucked into a multicourse meal that included everything from smoked salmon crepes to sea urchin consommé. The chef and his wife hung out behind the bar as I ate, telling me their life stories. We traded e-mail addresses, and I encouraged them to contact me if they ever came to America. "*Je suis très content*—I am very happy," the chef said at the end of the evening. So was I.

I continued to drift into experiences that I never would have had without strangers' help. I met a former Seiko board member who was celebrating his seventy-sixth birthday with his wife at a sushi restaurant called

Tuna People. The man, who spoke perfect English, gave me careful directions to a temple in his neighborhood north of Tokyo where monks put on a theatrical fire ritual called a *goma* ceremony several times a day. That night I asked the head sushi chef for his favorite dish, and after giving me both an unsolicited recommendation for an art museum and a plate of julienned raw squid, he presented me with a row of *nigiri* topped with uncooked mollusks. Following the suggestion of a young television host I met on the street, I sought out a public bath, and spent a morning soaking in a pool of steaming hot water backed by a mosaic of a blond mermaid. I asked an artsy-looking woman with highlighted hair and a fake leopard collar for her favorite lunch place and ended up in a Hawaiian-themed burger restaurant where the staff greeted me with "Aloha."

I never knew what might happen next. I went to the Electric Power Historical Museum, experimented with something called an aroma computer, visited a climbing gym, tried on a trendy wig, took photos of myself in a subterranean photo-booth arcade, and rode a subway train at rush hour (yes, that was actually a suggestion). I approached men, women, old people, young people, visitors from Taiwan and Australia, toy-store employees, Starbucks baristas, art students, bank tellers, and a young woman dressed as a bunny rabbit. And after each encounter I tried to do everything people told me to do.

If you'd talked to me before the trip, I'd have predicted that my experiment would be stressful. And indeed, if it had lasted longer, my excitement might well have turned to anxiety and annoyance. But instead, forbidding myself to plan for the future allowed me to be more grounded in the present; I felt a level of calm I rarely do in my normal life, where I'm supported not by strangers but by a loving network of family and friends. Why was this—and how could I bring the feeling home?

My last night in Tokyo fell on a Friday. I spent it in an area called the Golden Gai, a dense grid of alleys lined with tiny watering holes. The bar I entered had six seats and no standing room, and was presided over by a couple who led double lives as professional voice-over actors for cartoon characters. I chatted with the bartender as her husband sat silently in the corner eating rice crackers.

"What did you do today?" she asked in hesitant English. I'd told her about my project as the bar's other customers—three men in messy business suits—passed around my cards. When I announced that I'd visited a *sento*—a public bath—she laughed and interrupted me with a flood of Japanese that included two English words: "doctor fish."

It was as if I were listening to A.M. sports radio—I could tell she was speaking my language, but had no idea what she was saying.

"You know," she said, seeing my look of confusion. "Doctor fish." She made a nibbling motion with her fingers to demonstrate. "Eating your feet?"

Eventually, I figured out what she was talking about: a beauty treatment in which you stick your feet into a tank of water and let a special breed of fish nibble off your dead skin. It got its start as a treatment for psoriasis but now, apparently, was attracting a trendier clientele.

This was not what I'd anticipated doing on my last night in Tokyo. Karaoke, maybe. Feet-munching fish, not so much. But what the hell—I'd come this far on other people's suggestions. Why stop now? I had only one question: how to find a school of fish on call at 9:00 on a Friday night.

But that's the thing—once you realize you can ask people for help, it doesn't take long to find it. The owner gave the name of the spa to one of the businessmen, who made a call and found out the fish were not only on duty until 3:00 in the morning but were about a block from the bar. Excited, the owner led me around the corner and dropped me off in front of a glass window, through which

I could see a tank full of fish nibbling on someone's exposed toes.

I bought my ticket, rinsed my feet in the locker room, and plunked them into the tank. Then began the most ticklish ten minutes of my life as fish swam beneath and between my toes, quivering as they flicked their tiny mouths against my skin.

I doubt many philosophical treatises have been written in the company of doctor fish, but as a Japanese couple joined me in the tank and we giggled at one another (like love, tickling needs no translation), I had a thought. Learning to trust life is like learning to swim. First you flail, convinced you're going to drown. Then you notice that if you calm down, it's possible to tread water. And once you let go and just relax, you realize that the water was ready to support you all along.

Two for the Road

Justine van der Leun

—✳—

"We owe it to ourselves to go on adventures," my mother said. She was dressed in a kimono, drinking a glass of wine in bed. "I've always wanted to go to Santa Fe," I said, lying next to her in my pajamas, eating a bowl of spaghetti. We had no extended family and, because we were weirdos in our straight-and-narrow Connecticut town (I was a gangly twelve-year-old with a bad pageboy; she spent her free time painting Cubist windmills), few friends. "Santa Fe it is," my mother said, with a flourish of her arm. "What's stopping us?"

What should have stopped us was the soon-to-be discovered fact that my mother was a terrible vacation planner: dumbly adventurous, absentminded, and a little unlucky. We packed our bags for New Mexico, dreaming of winding mountain pathways and red deserts. We rose at dawn and hit the road. After a hearty diner breakfast, we turned off the highway, then off the main drag, and then, after traveling for miles, off the trail to take snapshots of each other triumphantly claiming the flat, desolate landscape as our own. When we returned to the car, it was locked: We peered through the window at the keys dangling from the ignition. "The coyotes will get us," I moaned. "Stand back!" yelled my wild-eyed mother as she ran toward the car, pitched her arm back, and threw a tiny boulder through the back driver's-side window.

Six months later, we toured the Northern California coast, staying in hippie hotels and making friends with people who owned Volkswagen buses. One day we strolled barefoot down an idyllic, unpopulated beach, gazing out at the cold, blue-green Pacific. "Hey," I said, hooking my arm in hers, "what's that big white thing floating in the water?" We got closer, dipped our toes in, and shielded our eyes from the sun. "It looks like a . . ." she began as her hair started to blow wildly. Several yards away, a heli-copter touched down and a team of men in yellow uniforms ran toward the water and hoisted out a dead, bloated body, wrapped it in a tarp, and strapped it on a stretcher. As they filed back toward the helicopter, a swollen foot poked out of the blanket, bobbing up and down. "I don't feel good," I said. "Me neither," she said.

One Christmas we drove through the lush and gloomy Irish countryside, taking tea at hillside manors and writing melancholy poems. In the night, my mother woke with a searing toothache. The cheery hotel clerk gave us a local's incomplete directions to the hospital ("I'm not sure what the street's name is, but it's by Malone's barn, and after that, take either your second, third, or fourth right"). We navigated our way down foggy, dark, curved roads, passing sign after sign with only large black dots on them. "What do those mean?" I asked, looking at my mother's white knuckles and imagining her as a racecar driver. "They mean someone died here."

Over the next five years, we rented a house in Maine that could have been a set for any movie adaption of a Stephen King novel and fled from a bed-and-breakfast owned by a New Age couple who beat drums in the backyard at dusk. My mother caught bronchitis in Paris; I fell off a horse in Utah.

When I was seventeen, we put on matching straw hats and boarded a charter plane to a tiny Caribbean island. It would be our last trip together for a while; I was leaving for college a few months later. "This will be tropical heaven," my mother said as the craft sputtered onto a small landing pad. "Strawberry daiquiris under an umbrella," I said. After traveling through dejected villages in the back of an open truck, we arrived at a cheerless hotel owned by an unfriendly clan. We trudged up the steps to a cement room with two cots and one mosquito net. When I stepped into the shower—differentiated from the rest of the room by a drain in the floor—I realized that to keep the water flowing, one had to hold on to a chain.

"I'm sorry," my mother said hopelessly.

After dark we walked along the shore toward the brightly lit resort in the distance—two dark silhouettes pulling heavy baggage along like smugglers. In a clumsy attempt at gaining speed, my mother swung her duffel in front of her and then fell face-first onto the beach. Instead of standing up, she flopped onto her back, sputtering sand. I looked at her, splayed out, lit by the moon, and began, against my will, to giggle. She joined me. "I really do try," she said. "Next time I start to plan a trip, stop me."

But I would never; I lived for our disastrous exploits. Other people messed up and had to answer to their mothers. My mother and I messed up together. Then we extracted ourselves from whatever predicament we'd gotten into. Other people, I imagined, lived boring lives, always explaining themselves and staying out of trouble. I preferred our terrible team of two, slightly bruised and plainly silly, getting into thrilling adventures that pushed the limits of absurdity—each one more delightful than the last.

Family Rituals

Marianne Gingher

—✳—

Every summer vacation, my children and I return to the
cottage my parents built in the Blue Ridge Mountains
thirty-five years ago. Our holiday is never properly launched
until, upon our arrival, just before dark, we scramble
through the sloping drapery of foliage and descend the
ridge behind the house to the meadow, where sinewy vines
hang like circus ropes from a canopy of trees. Parents and
children alike transform instantly. We cut vines from the
tangled roots and test them for swinging strength. Then,
holding tightly, we let ourselves loose upon the fragrant air,
soaring toward the distant twilit mountaintops, wreathed
in crowns of early stars.

The Year of Saying *Yes*

Patricia Volk

—✳—

I say no at the drop of a hat. I couch it as *knowing what is good for me*. Then I have dinner with my friend Louisa, who works in publishing. Late one afternoon, her editor says: "Louisa, I'm the keynote speaker tonight and I've got a scheduling conflict. You have to help me out."

"I found myself on a stage," Louisa reports, "with no idea what I was going to say. Then it occurred to me: *Louisa, you know more about this than they do.* And I started talking. And it was fine."

"I would have said no," I say.

"And wound up at home in bed with a book."

"What's wrong with that?"

"You're not living," Louisa says. "You're in a cocoon. You're not stretching."

Stretching? I have to keep stretching? Haven't I stretched enough? Didn't I support a (now ex-) husband through medical school while finishing my degree and raising two kids? Haven't I earned reading in bed with a bowl of Grape-Nuts for dinner? Peace, my new drug of choice.

Louisa and I kiss goodnight. Heading uptown, I argue with ME:

ME: "What's so good about a book in bed? Since when don't you take chances?"

I: "I'm relieved about what I'm missing."

ME: "But what are you missing? How do you know?"

I like arguing with myself. Everyone's a winner. By the time the bus drops me off, I've made a decision. Starting tomorrow, for one year, I'll strike no from my vocabulary. Tomorrow morning begins the Year of Saying *Yes*.

Congratulations! It's a Book!

Having a book published is like having a baby. No stretch marks, but it's yours to nurture. So *yes* to the Spencertown book fair in upstate New York, even though it costs $210 to rent a car and I sell only one book. And yes to the Caltech Athenaeum High Tea, even though I spend more time flying to Pasadena than *in* Pasadena. And yes to talking to my friend Patti's book club about my book. "I have a great idea," Patti says. "Since your novel deals with the importance of secrets, let's everybody tell a secret we've never told." I go first, and tell a secret involving my ninth-grade boyfriend, Harry, that once seemed devastating. Tincture of time makes this secret hilarious. Or so I think. But the women sit there frozen. Nobody else will tell theirs. I sell eleven books.

Broadway Debut

My friend Martin coproduces a show at the Symphony Space uptown. "Would you write something for it?" he asks.

I write a little ditty, changing the words to "How About You."

"Why don't you sing it?" Martin asks.

The big night arrives! It's time for my Broadway debut! So what if it's Broadway and Ninety-Fifth Street! There are two shows, six thirty and eight thirty. I print the lyrics on a doily in case I forget them. During the second show, I'm so excited, I forget to look at the doily and flub my lines. It doesn't matter. I read somewhere that when asked why he chose to spend his life on the stage, Sir Laurence Olivier replied by clapping. I get it.

A Blind Date

He picks me up in my lobby. We're both wearing blue-and-white gingham shirts! He's funny! Cute, too, even if I'm taller and outweigh him. At brunch he gets sad talking about his late wife. He won't eat. Walking me home, he asks, "What are you afraid of?"

"I'm afraid I'll never see a man in his underwear again," I say.

Right there in the street, he yanks the tail of his belt and starts to unzip. I scream. He says, "Now, if you hadn't yelled so loud, you would have seen a man in his underwear."

We take the long way home, walking miles through Central Park. He raves about his new TV equipment, then offers to come check out mine. Examining the setup, he says: "Do you have some time?" We walk more miles to a Best Buy, where he discusses my case with a salesman. Then we walk more miles back and he writes it all down.

Three days later, Blind Date breaks up with me before we hold hands. If I ever upgrade my TV, I'll know just what to get.

What Next?

The Year of Yes isn't over. Looming is a boat trip down the Hudson, cooking for a fund-raiser, a hat-making class, an ashram with my sister, two speeches, and participation in New York City International Pickle Day. When Yes Year is up, will I go back to no and Grape-Nuts? Maybe, but perhaps less of both. There isn't one thing I said yes to that I'm sorry I said yes to. And look what I would have missed. "No" means safety, and the numbing stasis that implies. I'm changed. The change has to do with the joy of being available to chance. There is a thrilling difference between being comfortable and being too comfortable. That difference makes you feel—there's no better word for it—radiant.

.

Sharing Delight

To get the full value of a joy you must have
somebody to divide it with.

—MARK TWAIN

Spread a Little Sunshine

Martha Beck

—✳—

I'm one of those people who just want to make everybody's day. I love humanity! Each man's joy is joy to me! Let's be honest, though: I can't spend *all* my time bringing bliss to others—I have work to do and bills to pay. Also, someone has to watch all six seasons of *Lost* on DVD, and to be blunt, I don't see you stepping up. But I digress.

My point is, I'm sure you, too, want to make other people's days, you with your six-page to-do list and your life-devouring job and that "will work for sleep" expression on your haunted little face. That's why I'm here to offer you not just seven ways to make someone else's day but seven ways to make someone else's day *without getting up.* You may need to dial a phone, but your torso can remain inert. That is my kind of altruism.

As you read the suggestions that follow, monitor yourself. If your mind says, *Great idea!* but your body says, *Too much work*, your body wins. Your mind will tell you it's virtuous to make someone's day in ways that make your own day stressful, but trust me—that just cancels out the overall benefit. This is simple math, people. Undertake these do-good strategies if and only if they feel exceptionally easy.

1. Feel good around other people.

Back in the '60s (and by that I mean the 1660s), a Dutch scientist named Christiaan Huygens realized that multiple pendulums mounted on the same wall always ended up swinging in perfect synchrony, even when he had set them in motion at different times. This phenomenon is called entrainment, and in my experience humans are just as likely to fall in sync as Huygens's clocks. At the very least, many neuroscientists believe that our so-called mirror neurons can foster our ability to empathize with the emotions we observe in others. One rage-aholic can fill an entire office with anger, while a truly happy person can lighten the mood for everyone around her. I once spent several hours in a room full of large sleeping dogs, who entrained me into such peace, I now count that uneventful afternoon as one of my life's highlights.

To make someone's day, all you have to do is stay physically near her while remaining in a state of contentment, humor, compassion, or calm. Try getting deeply happy around any loved one, acquaintance, or stranger. Refuse to let go of your good mood. You don't have to say or do anything else. Really. It'll make your day to see how easily you can make someone else's. And before you know it, you'll be soothing entire stressed-out crowds, like the ones you find at food courts and matador conventions.

2. Pretend people love you.

One of the statements that changed my life comes from spiritual teacher Byron Katie: "When I walk into a room, I know that everyone in it loves me. I just don't expect them to realize it yet." I'm by no means certain that everyone in every room loves me, but I've found that pretending they do works nicely when I want to make someone's day.

I spent much of my life wandering about armored against criticism and rejection, unaware that my wary defense appeared to others as inexplicable offense. And since everyone around me was also frightened, their defenses escalated the moment they encountered mine, which in turn ratcheted up to meet theirs, and so on. This emotional arms race drives people apart in every home, office, subway car, dentist's office, rice field, and square-dancing school on Earth. But pretending other people love you flips the vicious cycle into a virtuous one. Imagine how you'd enter a public space—say, a grocery store—if you knew without a doubt that everyone in it adored you. How would you move? How would you look at people? What would you say? Now imagine interacting with a loved one while feeling so sure of her infinite, unconditional acceptance that you had no need for reaffirmation. How would you behave? You'd probably lay down some of your armor. Then she would loosen hers. Then you'd relax even more, and so on and on and on. Try it right now—you can do so without getting up! Pretending someone loves you, right where you sit, will begin a day-making spiral of love.

3. Stop worrying about everyone.

Barbara sits before me fairly drowning in stress hormones. Her parents, who've come to the session with her, would do anything to eliminate her anxiety disorder and the panic attacks that go with it. Well, almost anything.

"We're so worried," says Barbara's mother, Janice.

"Mom, Dad," says Barbara, "please don't worry. It just puts pressure on me."

Janice's imploring eyes stay fixed on me. "What can we do?"

"Did you hear what she just said?" I ask.

"She's suffering." Dave, Barbara's dad, tells me.

"And what did she ask?"

"She needs to stop being so tense," says Janice.

"Actually, she asked you both to stop worrying," I say.

"Yes!" Barbara shouts.

"Well, of course we'll keep worrying," says Dave. "It's our job."

Barbara turns to me and whispers, "Help."

Mark this, gentle reader: Love and worry are not the same. (If you believe they are, I point you in the direction of blogger Jenny Lawson, who says: "A hug is like a strangle you haven't finished yet.") Think of someone you're worried about. Now replace worry with something else: creativity, perhaps, or singing or sudoku. I'm serious. It truly will make that person's day.

4. Advise people not to trust you.

One of the first things I tell new clients is not to trust me. Why should they? They don't know me. My job is to be trustworthy while telling them to put their trust where it belongs: in their own sense of truth. People often tell me that simply hearing this is enough to make their day. It's like taking spinach from a baby. (Whoever coined the phrase "taking candy from a baby" never had a baby.)

I also advise my loved ones, such as you, not to trust me. It's not that I'm pernicious or false—it's just that I'm fallible. If you trust me before trusting yourself, you'll rob us both of excellent counsel. So please don't trust anything I've written here unless it resonates as truth. Count on your instincts to keep you safe; they will. Doesn't that make your day?

5. Get someone else to help.

This may require a phone call, so put a phone near your Barcalounger. Then arrange for a third party—not yourself—to help the person whose day you're trying to make. Ask her what she needs: groceries delivered? a cleaning person to detail the kitchen? You needn't bankroll these services. Just be the one who makes the call.

Many are the days folks have made for me by enlisting help on my behalf. And I didn't have to feel guilty about burdening them, because I know that getting help for someone else is way less arduous than asking for help yourself. So go ahead, tell a nutritionist about your husband's constipation. Schedule a massage for your tightly wound best friend. Use that phone! Make that day!

6. Gossip positively.

To praise people to their faces is to be disbelieved. Most of us doubt or discredit positive feedback, chalking it up to politeness or brownnosing or other social convention. But what people say behind our backs really sticks. My life changed in an adolescent moment when I picked up a phone extension, not knowing the line was in use, and heard a conversation about me, me, me! I don't know what had gotten into the speakers—perhaps a great deal of what can only be called alcohol—but they were saying nice things about me. This not only made my day; it served as a foundation for emotional survival during some tough times thereafter.

Today, "mistakenly" copy someone on an e-mail about his best qualities. Leave positive comments about your children on notes "accidentally" scattered around the house. Admire people loudly to third parties when you know the admired are eavesdropping. Praise be.

7. Help a loved one play hooky.

This is an ethically gray area, so I would never say you should do it. I'm just hypothetically floating the crazy idea that one day you might happen to call in sick for someone you love ("Well, I think she'll keep the hand if the bacteria isn't antibiotic resistant, but it may be airborne. . . ."). Once she's freed from school or work, you could do something that would enrich her life forever. If that's the kind of thing you'd ever do. Which I would never suggest.

One day my friend Allen called in sick for his girlfriend Jenny, then took her scuba diving to a coral reef where he'd previously planted an engagement ring (okay, the diving involved getting up, but the calling didn't). Now Allen and Jenny are married. Does she regret the memos she failed to receive that day, the e-mails that waited twenty-four extra hours for an answer? She does not. Go figure.

A River Flows Through Us

Andrea Lee

—✳—

It was with a certain timidity that I began reading *Tom Sawyer* to my son, Charles. We live in Italy, and Charles, at twelve, with a smudge of nascent mustache, is one of those jaded bicultural kids now produced in such quantities by this shrinking planet: Half Italian on his father's side, half African-American on mine, he spends vacations in the States or traveling in Asia and Africa on a prodigiously stamped passport. He's a passionate reader, both in Italian and English, but compared to the sensational premises of the books he suddenly started devouring after *James and the Giant Peach*, *Tom Sawyer* seemed parochial, overly homespun, just plain small. Yet it seemed to me that a childhood without this book had a dead spot in it. I certainly didn't want him discovering it on a reading list for a college course entitled something like "Myth and Platonic Motif in Mark Twain."

So I resorted to trickery. One September morning, as we waited down at the end of our driveway for the bus from the International School to appear down the road, I pulled *Tom Sawyer* out of my pocket and said that though he was far too old to be read to, I needed practice for an upcoming book tour. As Charles gave me a cut-the-crap look, I added craftily that it would be useful in his often-described future career as dictator of the Western Hemisphere (twelve is a power-hungry age), as it was an American classic, a key to the hearts and minds of future subjects. Then I quickly started reading, not at the beginning, not even at the whitewashing episode, but at a point that instantly chimed with our immediate situation. "Monday morning found Tom Sawyer miserable. Monday morning always found him so—because it began another week's slow suffering in school."

My son, his eyes still clogged with sleep, sat hunched on his backpack on the ledge by the driveway, fiddling with a castor bean pod, the dog gnawing the toe of his running shoes, and listened to Tom's encounter with Huck

Finn on the way to school. "Say—what is dead cats good for, Huck?" "Good for? Cure warts with."

This is the kind of conversation that, in spite of contemporary distractions posed by YouTube, *Borat*, and André 3000, still sings to the youthful soul. I saw a glint in Charles's eye. "Mark the page," he commanded as the bus pulled up and he slouched out of the gate. And the next morning he asked me to start all over again, at the beginning.

After that, our morning appointments with *Tom Sawyer* became a ritual. I read aloud in the dank Northern Italian fog that rises off the Po River at the foot of our hill; on blazing clear days where the snowy line of the Alps gleams in the distance; in the rain, huddled soggily under an umbrella. As weeks passed and the oak and castor leaves turned brown and fell around us, and the school bus chugged past withering vineyards up the winding road, we made our leisurely way through the whitewashing, the pinch bug in church, Tom's staged death and glorious resurrection at his own funeral, the terror of Injun Joe, the ordeal with Becky Thatcher in the cave, the finding of the treasure. I recalled my own first reactions to the tale, which I read, like many other books, lying on a creaky glider on my sunporch in a black bourgeois

Philadelphia suburb that spiritually was nearly as far from Samuel Clemens's Missouri as our aerie in the Italian Piedmont hills.

My husband, who was born in Venice during the Second World War and whose childhood experience of Americans was mainly limited to Gary Cooper movies and a standing maternal order to avoid GIs and their offers of chocolate, was pleased by our reading, and confessed that *Tom Sawyer* had been his favorite book as a boy. When Charles and I challenged him as to what he remembered, he listed everything precisely: whitewash, funeral, Becky, cave, treasure. He said it reminded him of days he'd spent on the lagoon with his friends, messing around in boats, fishing, swimming in canals (Venice was cleaner then). "I always thought of the Mississippi as looking something like the Giudecca," he added dreamily.

It's well known that great books are universal, but I was struck by the ability of this slender tale to delight any reader just on the verge of growing up. One reason it does so, of course, is that it focuses on the friction between the safe, constrained world of childhood and the terrible joys of mature freedom, lawless adventure, romantic love, the heroic pleasure of cutting a figure in the eyes of the world. I found unexpectedly touching the scene in which Tom and his friend Joe Harper, who have run off to live in a boys' paradise on a Mississippi island, begin to sicken of freedom, to feel the pangs of desire for rules, home, the boundaries imposed by their mothers. "Swimming's no good," Joe says. "I don't seem to care for it, somehow, when there ain't anybody to say I sha'n't go in." I've seen it many times at the end of the day, how boys who at the height of their energy seem like supermen, with their alarming sophistication, their rambunctious strength, their overweening need to push limits, suddenly, almost pathetically, ask to be children again.

Both Charles and I sat riveted the morning I read Clemens's chilling expansion into oratory as he describes the dying villain's futile attempts to gather drinking water from a dripping stalactite. "That drop was falling when the Pyramids were new; when Troy fell; when the foundations of Rome were laid; when Christ was crucified . . . when Columbus sailed. . . . It is falling now; it will still be falling when all these things shall have sunk down the afternoon of history, and the twilight of tradition, and been swallowed up in the thick night of oblivion."

Some time later, Charles said: "You forget that all

this stuff is happening to just one boy in a tiny little town. It's a big story."

Big. That's just what I thought, and at the end of our reading, I felt triumphant, pleased that an American river, a small-town tale, could reach over time and space.

The Snug Life

Celia Barbour

—✳—

The nicest thing I ever did for my single self was to buy an apartment in New York City's West Village. I'd been slumming it for seven years, living in a fifth-floor walk-up tenement, and one day I decided that a proper home was no longer a self-indulgence. I was as real a grown-up as I'd ever be, and deserved a real place.

My lovely one-bedroom apartment had a park out front, trees out back, a working fireplace, and, at 575 square feet, was just big enough for me and my cat, and the occasional dinner party with friends. No sooner had I settled in than I met my husband, Peter, and he moved in. We felt cozy; life was sweet. Sometimes at night, we'd sit on the stoop with two jelly jar glasses of Scotch and watch the people passing by. A year and a half later, George was born, and I dusted off an old baby basket and placed it on the floor beside our bed. When Henry came along sixteen months after that, he laid claim to the basket and George was reassigned to our walk-in closet, which Peter, a proficient carpenter, had transformed into a nursery. Then Sidonie was born. Switch-switch-switch: George to a trundle bed (built by Peter) that rolled under our bed, Henry into the closet, the baby girl in the basket. And so we lived, snug as mice, for a very happy little while.

Last year we moved into a house. Built in 1900, it has three stories, eight rooms, and five bathrooms, plus an attic that smells like heat and a basement that smells like mold. It has doors that close and hallways separating one room from another, places to talk privately on the phone and to do yoga in the morning without having my torso straddled by a kid who has suddenly perceived my untapped potential as a hobbyhorse. Our house is not big, at least by contemporary standards, because it has no superfluous rooms devoted to leisure or grandeur—no family room, for example, and no great room cowering beneath a cathedral ceiling. We have just the basic LR,

DR, BR, K, study. Which is fine, despite the fact that the kids are growing like corn, because all our rooms are living rooms, by which I mean we live in them all. The only time I find myself wishing for more square footage is when I am overwhelmed by stuff—books, vases, wrapping paper, hand-me-downs waiting to be grown into, chairs—and daydream about building an addition where the flotsam could comfortably reside. Then I think: "Don't be crazy, Celia." A home is a place to do things, not store things. It's not meant to house your possessions, but your life.

And it turns out that our lives together are quite compact. Yes, during the day we each might spiral off into the wide, wild world—the kids at school studying China or peninsulas, bicycling around the neighborhood or sledding down the hill, Peter and I doggedly pursuing our careers. But back at home, we draw close, this habit of being in one another's presence ingrained. Unconsciously, we collect in the same room, even if we are each doing our own things—the boys building LEGO speedboats, Peter replying to e-mails, me reading, Sidonie communicating quietly to her stuffed animals. We may not be interacting with one another at all. But having started out like pieces of a single puzzle nestled together so neatly, we still return to that familiar configuration. As individuals we may be big, but as a family, we are really very small.

Married, with Other People's Children

Veronica Chambers

All my adult life I have had a passion for what I call OPC: other people's children. I love introducing my nieces and nephews and kid friends to my favorite books, jump rope tricks, and rhymes. I try to have my own relationship with the children in my life. I write them letters, call them for playdates, go to recitals and plays. And as I've gotten into my thirties, I've upped the ante. It took me six months, for example, to find a Hawaiian tiki hut/lemonade stand (and a pair of matching grass skirts) to ship to my nieces in Philadelphia for Christmas. The year before, I had given my nephews a laptop. I've opened 529 savings funds for their college educations, which turned out to be easy—with a minimum of a twenty-five-dollar monthly contribution,

I could set up an automatic withdrawal from my bank account, and after a while, that fifty dollars or seventy-five dollars didn't hurt at all.

One year I sent my nephew Frederick to football camp at the University of Pennsylvania. He comes from a rough neighborhood, and at the time he was thirteen and already getting in trouble with gangs. He's a talented football player, hence the camp, but more than anything I wanted him to get a glimpse of college life. I loved driving him up to the Penn dorms and seeing him fall in love with campus life. The summer after that, I sent Frederick's brother, Jesse, to mountain-biking camp in New Hampshire. I was looking for a place where Jesse wouldn't feel like a Fresh Air Fund kid but would still get a glimpse of a different life. Jesse spent two weeks biking down ski trails, riding through mud. He also learned how to pitch a tent and surf, and I became the coolest aunt ever.

This past summer, Jesse came to stay with us for seven weeks. For years we'd been finding programs for our nephews, writing checks. But having Jesse live with us for almost two months took things to a new level. He had schoolwork to do and book reports to write on his break. We had to learn how to be disciplinarians. We also had to organize his social schedule. The first day I had two twelve-year-old boys running through my house, I thought I was going to lose my mind. Then came the day when I had four twelve-year-old boys running through the house, and I realized I had no mind left to lose. And that was more than okay. I loved it.

There were hard moments: times when Jesse let us know that we were *not* his parents and we could rot in hell for all he cared. There were doors slammed, and there were tears. Both my husband and I were trying to feel for the boundaries. In the end, we decided we could only do what real parents actually do: wing it and pray that when we got it wrong, we weren't doing irreparable damage. And I'm guessing we didn't, because the last night Jesse was with us, he was invited to a party where all the cool kids he'd met over the summer were going to be hanging out—and he chose to stay home and hang out with us instead.

After Jesse left, Jason and I had the conversation we've had a zillion times. We would like to have a family, and we would really like to adopt. But our nieces and nephews are getting older. Each year these kids become more independent and interesting. I have fantasies of taking my nieces to Paris and my nephews to Tokyo, of showing them all the places I've been and loved. Some days Jason and I think, *Why should we bother reaching into the ether for children we do not know, when there are already these half-dozen children who've staked their claim in our world?* Again and again, we get stuck there. We love our friends' kids. We love our nieces and nephews. We love being the relief-pitcher parents. But the problem with other people's children is that you have to give them back.

Then again, a week after my nephew went home, I walked into his room, which had reverted to our guest room, and for the first time all summer, it did not smell like eau de twelve-year-old boy. I put on a pair of stilettos and a sexy blouse, and my husband took me to dinner, alone, for the first time all summer. The waiter arrived with a lovely bottle of sauvignon blanc and we raised our glasses to toast the best part of OPC: freedom.

You're Welcome

Lauren F. Winner

—✳—

Last month my friend Mary and her sister came to visit from Virginia. Their three-day stay was my great chance to show that, though exiled in Manhattan, I could still haul out the Southern hospitality. I wasn't sure that I and my tiny, dust-bunnied, grad-student apartment were up to it, and it turned out that we weren't, quite. I had to ask my guests to bring their own towels, because I owned only two. (Well, now I own four: Mary sent me a pair of fluffy 110-ply blue ones as a thank-you gift.)

I grew up on biblical stories about hospitality. In Genesis, Abraham goes out of his way to welcome three guests, strangers all. They turn out not to be weary, rumpled travelers but angels who have come to tell the childless

Abraham and Sarah that they'll soon have a son. This story is echoed in the Gospels, which tell of two men who encounter a stranger on the road to Emmaus. As they walk, the two men invite the stranger to join them for dinner, and while breaking bread they realize their guest is the risen Jesus.

Hospitality is supposedly something we do for others, but whenever I have guests (even those who don't buy me towels or turn out to be angels or deities), I feel like I'm reaping the benefits. Hospitality involves sharing an intimate, private place, and letting someone in shows trust. It shows that we're committed to lasting relationships with our friends, not just quick coffees when convenient.

If Mary and her sister had stayed in a hotel when they came to New York, we would have met up for dinner one night, but I wouldn't have spilled my romantic woes to her at 7:45 A.M. while her sister was showering and I was curling my hair. I wouldn't have counseled Mary, over late-night tea, about whether she should continue to scrape by as a writer or search for a teaching job. There simply wouldn't have been time.

My mother, a fine hostess when she sets her mind to it, rarely has overnight guests because she feels she has to turn her house into *Martha Stewart Living* to accommodate them. She stocks the kitchen with home-baked goodies, dusts floorboards that were dusted two days before, and buys new hand towels, soaps, and lotions for the guest bathroom. In the 1957 edition of *Etiquette*, Emily Post describes the endless trials of the perfect hostess: If the cook leaves, the hostess will have to organize a last-minute picnic. Unless she "is actually unable to stand up," a hostess must keep any physical ailments hush-hush. "The ideal hostess must have so many perfections . . . that were she described in full, no one seemingly but a combination of seer and angel could ever hope to qualify."

The first step to reviving hospitality is redefining it. I can't imagine having time even to shop for dinner, much less cook it, but I can order in exotic Swedish food that Mary and her sister won't find in Charlottesville. I can scan my crowded bookshelves for the titles they'll enjoy and leave them on the bedside table. And I can make sure Mary's favorite Irish tea is in my cabinet. Guests aren't looking for five-course meals. They're looking for a little comfort away from home, a firm mattress, a warm welcome. And what they offer in return is the incomparable joy of closeness.

The Joan Show

Jessica Winter

—*—

My husband saw her first, on a cold December afternoon. The veterinary clinic down the street from our apartment sometimes parks stray kittens in its front window; a scrawny calico, with fur like dandelion fluff, was mewling at him through the glass, as if he were an errant teenager who'd just plowed his bicycle into her parked car. He called me; I hustled over. When I picked her up, her body relaxed instantly, as if she'd been rigid with anticipation a long time and now could finally breathe easy. She hooked her tiny white paws over my shoulder and snuggled close. She purred dreamily. She sighed a little kitten sigh. Half an hour later, she was in our apartment.

Now, years later, that moment at the clinic remains the

one and only time I have ever gotten a hug from my cat. First impressions to the contrary, Joan—my husband named her Joan, as in Didion, "for her poise and figure"—does not like being cuddled. When she submits to petting, it is often in the wriggly, distressed manner of a small child surrendering to the attentions of a grizzled old aunt with an ashtray kiss.

Failure has touched much of my tenure as Joan's coguardian. I failed to teach her to fetch. I failed to convince her that the couch is not a potato that needs peeling. I failed to sell her on her water bowl. (Faucets only.)

I can't change Joan, or even slightly modify her. Instead, she has changed me. It never occurred to me before that I could love another creature so much without expecting reciprocation. I must be content to admire Joan slightly from afar, as one might admire a famous actor or athlete. The upside is that I have year-round tickets (excellent seats, too) for *The Joan Show*: spinning leaps through the air at a dangled dish towel; vertical sprints along our living room walls; heroic combat-crawl missions into my parents' garden, from which she emerges with voles attached to her claws like finger puppets.

And once in a while she'll curl up beside us at bedtime, or offer a friendly headbutt. Maybe I'll come home from work and she'll trot up the hall to greet me, cooing like a turtledove. Or maybe I'll be crying over something stupid and she'll place a comforting paw on my knee. Come to think of it, she does that dainty paw-pat every time, and it always makes me laugh through my tears.

Come On, Get Happy

It is not easy to find happiness in ourselves,
and it is not possible to find it elsewhere.

—AGNES REPPLIER

Pleasure 101

Gretchen Reynolds

—✳—

If you're used to thinking of happiness as an elusive, un-attainable quality that arrives only when everything is ab-solutely perfect (good luck with that), you'll be glad to hear that you've got it all wrong. As it turns out, pleasure can be had quite readily—provided you're ready to try a few of these simple steps:

- **Chocolate can be a taste of ecstasy.** It not only releases good-vibe brain chemicals but also feels pleasant in the mouth. It speaks to us, culturally, of reward and indul-gence.
- **Then there's music.** Try listening to a soothing piece, a song that calms you. Close your eyes. Your pulse

should slow and your muscles loosen. Not happening? Put on classical, folk, rock, soul, hip-hop, reggaeton—whatever appeals. Let the music transport you, make you forget where you are, how long you've been listening, and . . . you were saying something about troubles?

- **Go outside.** Walk or drive to the nearest park or beach, away from human hubbub. Sit quietly. Listen for finches, gulls, the whisper of a breeze, the bubble and whoosh of a stream. If someone is with you, reach for that person's hand. Smile. Say nothing. Let the birds chorus.

- **Look at something beautiful.** Watching CNN's war-and-natural-disaster coverage, while good for your civic knowledge, won't do much for your sense of well-being. But there's an antidote: Switch to a slow, soothing nature show. Lush landscapes and quiet scenes of ponds and streams quell distress. Find a room with a view, especially of trees, grass, and sky. Any view will help, even of a parking lot. To find pleasure, look at life.

- **Remember.** Memories often carry melancholy, too, and that emotion also is bound up in our sense and our joys. Ask any mother of grown children who sniffs a newborn's peachy-sweet head. Her pleasure will be plaited with loss. It won't necessarily be any less buoying for that, though.

- **Smell things!** Scents can send you. Pleasure is wrapped up with remembrance, as Marcel Proust knew but neuroscientists are only beginning to understand. The smells that give you the most pleasure are tied to your loves and longings and your life's experiences. Think back to when you were happiest. Was it your wedding night, or the day you got the job of your dreams? How did that moment smell? Was your husband wearing a freshly laundered shirt? Did your new employer have roses in her office? Do some detective work. Visit fragrance counters and flower shops. Close your eyes. Breathe deep. Keep a journal of the smells that unexpectedly transport you. Then re-create them. Turn off the lights, lie down, and inhale a freshly picked rose, or bury your nose in one of your husband's shirts, preferably one he's just taken off as he slips into bed beside you.

Could You Be Happier?

Dan Baker, Ph.D.

—*—

It might seem a little mood-ring era to suggest taking a happiness quiz. Many people, however, are "so used to being unhappy that they barely notice it," says psychologist Dan Baker, Ph.D., coauthor of What Happy People Know. *"It's like living next to railroad tracks: After a while, you don't hear the trains." Using the latest research, Baker has devised an emotional checkup based on his theory that happiness develops from a number of internal qualities, including courage, love, humor, altruism, and a sense of freedom and purpose. Although it's impossible to quantify precisely how happy a person is, this quiz will give you a general idea of where you fall on the spectrum. Start by choosing how often you agree with the following statements.*

Never [N]; Infrequently [I]; Sometimes [S]; Frequently [F]

1. I believe my life will truly begin when the right person or circumstances come along.

   [N] [I] [S] [F]

2. I feel best when I give unconditionally.

   [N] [I] [S] [F]

3. When I think about people in my life, I focus on those who have hurt or disappointed me.

   [N] [I] [S] [F]

4. When I think about people in my life, I focus on those I care about and love.

   [N] [I] [S] [F]

5. There is not enough time for taking care of me.

   [N] [I] [S] [F]

6. I've helped myself through difficult times with a positive attitude.

   [N] [I] [S] [F]

7. I take myself very seriously.

   [N] [I] [S] [F]

8. I believe it's up to me to find meaning in my life.

    [N] [I] [S] [F]

9. When things don't go well, I feel trapped or overwhelmed.

    [N] [I] [S] [F]

10. Although life's circumstances change, my beliefs and capabilities will allow me to survive and thrive.

    [N] [I] [S] [F]

11. Who wouldn't rather receive a gift than give one?

    [N] [I] [S] [F]

12. There is a spiritual power that I can turn to for comfort whenever I need to.

    [N] [I] [S] [F]

13. There are events in my life that have left me forever scarred and impaired.

    [N] [I] [S] [F]

14. Life is a big joke, and it's often at my expense.

    [N] [I] [S] [F]

15. Fear keeps me from standing up for what I believe in.

    [N] [I] [S] [F]

16. I've grown—emotionally, spiritually—through difficult and painful events.

    [N] [I] [S] [F]

17. Without enough money or love, I can't feel secure.

[N] [I] [S] [F]

18. I make taking care of my health a priority.

[N] [I] [S] [F]

19. People hurt my feelings.

[N] [I] [S] [F]

20. Life is good, and I appreciate what I have.

[N] [I] [S] [F]

21. I'm unclear about the purpose and meaning of my life.

[N] [I] [S] [F]

22. What matters most is enjoying relationships.

[N] [I] [S] [F]

23. I have too much to do.

[N] [I] [S] [F]

24. I feel fulfilled.

[N] [I] [S] [F]

Scoring

- For every time you answered "sometimes," give yourself a 2.
- For even-numbered questions: "never" and "infrequently" get a 1, and "frequently" gets a 3.

- For odd-numbered questions: "never" and "infrequently" get a 3, "frequently" gets a 1.
- Add up your total.

Results

- 50 to 72: Congratulations! Consider yourself a happy person.
- 30 to 49: You're not miserable, but your sunny side could use a nudge. Think about your strengths and the activities you love; focus more of your life on them. Obvious? Yes—but so is sleeping an extra hour when you're tired: The trick is to actually *do* it.
- 29 or less: You could be getting so much more from life. Is your language—including the dialogue in your head—destructive? Over time, a little lingo substitution can gradually lift the mood. Is your first impulse to find fault? Try seeking out possibilities instead. Do you know any happy people? If so, what can you learn from them? When something bad happens, do you fall apart? That old cliché about finding strength through adversity is a golden rule for happy people. Finally, are you assuming that money, power, or status will bring you satisfaction—or that everything will be great when someone else changes? If so (and you get points for being

honest), try shifting your focus inward and take responsibility for your emotions. Bottom line, and you've probably heard this every third day of your life, but there's a reason for that: Only you can make yourself happy.

Cheers!

Lise Funderburg

—✳—

Many of us have a hunch—though it hasn't been proven beyond the shadow of a doubt—that the only category of humanity more annoying than street mimes is optimists. You know them: sunny Pollyannas in denial about the world's harsh realities, skipping along, head in the clouds, and no doubt (we hope) about to step in something unpleasant.

But optimism is much more than a reckless chirping through our days. According to experts, it's a high-voltage power tool in the life-skills toolbox. Researchers have characterized it as everything from a coping mechanism to a physical patterning of neurobiological pathways established in our earliest years.

Optimists know how to bounce back. They can see a setback as temporary, changeable. If an optimist encounters a recipe she can't make work, she's likely to perceive the failure as external and temporary ("I'm having an off day"), while the pessimist makes it internal and indelible ("I'll never learn to cook"). Victories are just the reverse: Optimists think of them as permanent and far-reaching; pessimists think of them as fleeting and situation-specific.

If you nurture a sense of possibility and the expectation of positive results, you're more likely to have a life in which possibilities are realized and results are positive. You'll have a better chance of being promoted, fighting off the cold that's been going around, and attracting people to you—platonically and otherwise. Pessimistic people are two to eight times more at risk for depression. And researchers have found that optimists are less likely to develop cancer or to die from heart disease.

Almost everyone can learn to be more optimistic, even if that means distorting reality. You can also begin to recognize and catalog the negative messages you give yourself, then dispute those thoughts as if debating an external foe. Gradually, the new responses become automatic.

According to some researchers, each of us has a

happiness "set point." We've each been dealt a happiness hand, some of us with higher cards than others. But we can increase our potential for joy by taking steps to get involved with people, causes, and ideas. One of the hallmarks of depression is self-absorption. And so optimism, with its emphasis on seeking and seeing what's good outside of ourselves and in the world, helps us take those steps.

Taking a Chance on Joy

Roger Housden

—✳—

You know those moments when nothing special is happening—maybe you wake up early one morning to the sound of a thrush outside the window, or perhaps to the whir of the traffic below your apartment—and a smile spreads over your face for no reason? You feel different, aware of an ease in your body that wasn't there before.

With hindsight, I've come to see that moments like these happen when I have forgotten myself. When, for a moment or two, the plotline of my life dissolves and I am just where I am, without the responsibility of playing the lead in my own fascinating story. My dramas, worries, and concerns, my aspirations and hopes and fears, fall away.

I have no agenda, nothing I want to do, nothing I want to alter or improve upon. The air is lighter, and so am I.

But then, the world is not easy. It can take all our time and attention to avoid hitting the shallows or landing on the rocks that seem to be such an intrinsic part of the human experience. We have only to look at our lives, or those of people we know, to see that pain and suffering strike even the most fortunate. So who has time to forget what we're meant to be doing and where we're meant to be going? Life is a serious business, and someone needs to be there to steer the ship. What is the use of gazing out the window, doing nothing?

I think our difficulty in accessing happiness lies in large part right there: We are usually preoccupied with being useful—doing something with an outcome in mind, rather than being open to where we are at this moment—and we are largely convinced that nobody goes to heaven for having a good time. We think pain is virtuous. Suffering can be a great purifier, a forger of character, no doubt about that; but happiness can take us into the wide world beyond our own self-preoccupations. It can join us to the trees, to other people, to cows and to stones and to the living pulse of humankind itself. It can join us to the china mug of tea in our own hand. Strange, then, that it should seem so fleeting.

Joy is weightless, light as ether; you communicate it less in words than by a savor you leave in the air. It is our natural state. It is the feeling of who we are when we are most at home in ourselves. It means there is nothing else to add to what we already have, or to who we already are.

Why would we ever want to resist it? I suspect it's because not having a big story to tell can feel undefended, tender. There's not so much to hold on to, less substance in our identity when we are happy, in the sense of wanting nothing. Happy isn't so interesting to talk about as sad, and it doesn't have a through line—it is for now, without any future in mind. Most of our talking is about the past or the future, and when we are happy, we are in neither.

The world is so full of sorrows, you might say; how can we deserve or dare to feel simple delight? How can we afford *not* to, the poet Jack Gilbert asks in his poem "A Brief for the Defense." Sorrow is everywhere, he says; people are suffering deeply all over the world. Yet the women in the brothels of Bombay laugh out loud, and women at the well smile and sing even as their neighbor is wasting away. If we refuse our happiness, we diminish in some way their deprivation. No, "We must risk delight . . . / We must have / the stubbornness to accept our gladness in the ruthless / furnace of this world."

Stop Whining!

Roxane Gay

—✳—

I have lived in rural America for nine years, first in Michigan, where I was getting my Ph.D.; then in central Illinois; and now in Indiana, where I am a professor. In a place where most people have lived the whole of their lives, I feel like a stranger—someone on the outside looking in.

There are few things I enjoy more than complaining about my geographic isolation. I'm a vegetarian, so there's nowhere to go out for a nice dinner that doesn't involve a fifty-mile drive. I'm black, so there's nowhere to get my hair done that doesn't involve *another* fifty-mile drive. I'm single, and the dating options are, at times, rather grim. The closest major airport is two hours away.

I recite these complaints to my parents, my brothers,

my friends. I complain in long, pathetic e-mails and essays. It just feels so damn good to say, *I am mildly miserable! Behold my misery!* Alas, suffering offers more nobility than joy.

Sometimes it seems like complaints are the lingua franca among my friends. We are all dissatisfied with something. Back in Illinois, my friends complained about the train to Chicago and how it's never on time; my friends in bigger cities complain about the expensive rent and strange smells on the subway; my married friends complain about their partners; my single friends complain about the wretchedness of dating. I cannot even get into my friends with kids.

Complaining allows us to acknowledge the imperfect without having to take action—it lets us luxuriate in inertia. We all have grand ideas about what life would be like if only we had *this*, or did *that*, or lived *there*. Perhaps complaining helps bridge the vast yawn between these fantasy selves and reality.

But it also makes me lose sight of things. While I may not love where I live, there are plenty of people who are proud to call this place home. Recently, at a party with some colleagues, I was going on and on about everything I couldn't stand about our town when I noticed that they were mostly silent and shifting uncomfortably. That humbling moment forced a shift in *me*.

Complaining may offer relief, but so does acceptance. There is no perfect place. There is no perfect life. There will always be something to moan about. By focusing on my grievances, I risk missing out on precious, startling moments of joy. Those times when, during a long drive home from the airport, I stare out at the prairie flatness, the breathtaking shades of green as tender buds of corn push their way through freshly tilled soil; at the wooden barns, their paint peeling and faded; and at all manner of farm equipment—massive, but there is poetry in how these behemoths rumble across the land. When I get home, I stand on my balcony and look up into the night sky and see all the stars. And I know that I have absolutely nothing to complain about.

Dare to Play

Brené Brown

—✳—

A few years ago, I noticed in my research that wholehearted people—my term for men and women with the courage to be vulnerable and live their lives "all in"—shared something else, too: They goofed off. They spent time doing things that to me seemed frivolous, like gardening and reading. I couldn't really wrap my head around it—were they slackers? Then one day, while I watched my kids jump on the trampoline in our backyard, it hit me: Wholehearted adults play.

A researcher I know describes play as time spent without purpose. To me this sounds like the definition of an anxiety attack. I feel behind if I'm not using every last moment to be productive, whether that means working, cleaning the house, or taking my son to baseball practice. But I can't ignore what the research (mine and others') tells us: Play—doing things just because they're fun and not because they'll help achieve a goal—is vital to human development. Play is at the core of creativity and innovation. Play can mean snorkeling, scrapbooking, or solving crossword puzzles; it's anything that makes us lose track of time and self-consciousness, creating the clearing where ideas are born.

Which means it's a mistake to restrict play to vacations. There are plenty of ways to incorporate it into your everyday life:

- **Create a play list.** Write down three activities you could do for hours on end. Mine are reading, editing photos on my computer, and playing Ping-Pong with my family.
- **Now carve out time on your calendar.** Even when I'm busiest, I schedule unstructured time. It's important to protect playtime the way you protect work, church, or PTA meetings.
- **Play well with others.** When my husband and kids made their own play lists, we realized that our usual vacations,

which involved sightseeing, weren't really anyone's idea of play. So now we go places where we can hike, swim, and play cards—things that make us all our most silly, creative, and free-spirited selves.

Uncrumpling My Face

Catherine Newman

My son, Ben, peers over my shoulder at the photograph in my hand. "I love that picture," he says—and of course he does. All he sees is his peachy six-year-old self in the foreground, blurred with happiness and dancing with his little sister, pantsless and laughing. Who wouldn't smile to see them? Well, someone wouldn't—whatever that thing is in the background, hunched in its robe over a coffee mug. Even from here you can't miss my scowl lines, like the angry stomp of a pterodactyl foot between the eyes. It's the kind of face that would make you pedal your bike faster if you saw it in a window from the street.

Listen, I'm a feminist. I'm not vain. But I mind looking like a bitch.

Remember Dorian Gray? How he remained baby smooth while an old oil painting of him magically wrinkled up into oblivion? I'm like that, but on Opposite Day: Somewhere in the attic there must be a smooth portrait of me, my face a glossy bisque to reflect the contentment I feel inside. But my actual face looks as if it's been pressed onto the front of my head after first getting wadded up like a Big Mac wrapper.

"I'm getting Botox," I joke to my husband, Michael. "But not so I'll look younger—just to prevent me from scowling at all of you."

I am totally kidding—and then, suddenly, I'm not. What if I were physically unable to pull my face into negativity? Perhaps I would be paralyzed away from my own bouts of bad temper. Studies have proved this, or something like it: A facial expression doesn't simply reflect your moods; it actually shapes them. Frown and you feel sad; laugh and your spirits lift. Is mood enhancement one of Botox's promises? I can't say, since I'm too proud and broke to consider it seriously. Also the word "botulism" unnerves me. Instead I choose a moisturizer from the mile of products at the drugstore, but massaging it into my rutted forehead just gives me a scattering of pimples.

Then, in the bath one evening, I suddenly remember the *Old Farmer's Almanac* I paged through in the tub as a child—in particular, the ads for those old-fashioned "Frownies" beauty patches, a kind of Scotch tape for the face, which pulls your wrinkles apart in hopes they'll stay flat. The company still exists, it turns out, the Web site offering smiling headshots of women and guarantees of happy results. Plus they're cheap. I order some. You're supposed to separate them at their perforations, lick them, and stick them to your skin. All in all they are about as high-tech as pebbles or cheese.

My family understands the beige triangle to be a symbol of my renewed benevolence. When I sigh one night over a pot of borscht, Ben asks if he can get me a Frownie the way you might offer aspirin to someone with a headache. My daughter, Birdie, her own face aglow with toddler sweetness, touches it with a serious fingertip and asks, "If I pull this off, then you'll be grumpy?"

Well, yes, maybe. Because however bizarre this ritual may be, it's working. Taped into placidity, I can't really scowl. The more I don't scowl, the more my family grins back. And here's the only part of my strange experiment that *isn't* crazy: The more the people I love most smile at me, the happier I feel.

Don't Go Changing

Beth Levine

—*—

Recently, a friend asked me if I'd ever been to Israel. Before I could even open my mouth, she added slyly, "Oh, that's right. You can't get on a plane." I think she was trying to be funny.

There was a time when I would have died a thousand deaths: *She knows my dirty secret; she's making fun of me; she thinks I'm pathetic; I am, in fact, pathetic.* This time, however, I stopped the tape in my head and played a new one. It said, *Everyone has a screw loose somewhere, and having a thing about planes happens to be mine.*

You have no idea how hard I've worked to get here.

I've been a fearful flyer since grade school. Once I grew up, I could white-knuckle a flight, but the months leading up to it were full of panic attacks, sleepless nights, canceling, and rebooking. (And, once we landed, constant worry about the flight back.) Along with fear came self-loathing: I was defective, weak, chickenshit. Why could everyone else just *do* this? My last flight was in 1986, a quick and uneventful trip on the shuttle from New York to Boston. I haven't flown since.

Oh, I tried, I tried. Cognitive behavioral therapy, classes, tranquilizers, meditation, workbooks. Everything seemed to make it worse. I once got myself admitted to a Yale University airplane phobia study. My first meeting was scheduled for—wait for it—September 11, 2001. When the World Trade Center was falling, I was getting ready to leave for a fear-of-flying intake. Needless to say, I didn't go to the meeting. I didn't go to any subsequent meetings. I gave up, but the self-flagellation didn't stop: *Look at all the amazing experiences you could be having, you big weenie!*

So I decided to go have some. On a whim, I auditioned for a show at a community theater. Much to my surprise, I got the part, then another that involved singing and dancing (neither of which I do particularly well). All my friends asked, "Aren't you terrified?" That stopped me short. I, the Queen of Panic, had zero anxiety about—and took much joy in—doing something most people fear. In other words:

There were things I could do that other folks couldn't! Maybe I wasn't going to see the Taj Mahal anytime soon, but how many of my friends could blithely play a ninety-year-old obese ex-vaudevillian in front of an audience without an ounce of fear?

Life wasn't passing me by because I couldn't get on a plane—it was passing me by because I was obsessing about what I couldn't do instead of rocking the things I could. *Fly or don't fly*, I thought, *but don't waste another minute whining about it.*

Not long after, while poking around a gift shop, I found a striated brown agate with a word engraved in it: gratitude. It took my breath away. That one word distilled my shift in attitude. For me to pity myself, not to celebrate the talents, strengths, and opportunities I have—well, that would be ungrateful. The rock now sits on my dresser. I think about its message every day. I am not my fears, and my fears are not me. My world is way bigger than that.

Ask Away

Elizabeth Gilbert

—✳—

One morning in 1993, I walked into the offices of a famous magazine in New York City and asked for a job as a writer. I had no appointment, no experience, and not a single published article to my name. But I'd had an epiphany: Nobody was ever going to knock on my door and say, "We understand a talented writer lives here, and we'd like to help her with her career!" No. *I* would have to go knocking on doors.

So I did. I just walked in off the street and asked to be hired as a reporter. And guess what? It didn't work! (Of course it didn't work; they weren't dummies, and I was totally unqualified—jeez, how do you think the world operates, people?) But I still think of it as one of the most important moments of my life because it was the boldest. When I went home that day, I was still broke and obscure, but at least I knew I was brave. I wouldn't have to suffer the pain of knowing I hadn't tried.

Nearly eight hundred years ago, the Persian mystic poet Rumi wrote, "You must ask for what you really want." He saw asking as a sacred duty, and I think he was right—not because your wishes will be granted automatically (they won't), but because the mere act of saying aloud "This is who I am and what I've come for" seems to awaken a powerful force within. By articulating your wish, you're making an announcement that you're serious about bringing the next great thing—and real, lasting happiness—into your life.

The hurdle, however, is that asking for what you really want—whether it's a job as a writer or a discount on tires—can be difficult. Especially for women. First of all, you must *know* what you really want, which can be hard if you were raised to please others. Secondly, you must believe that what you want is worthy—again, a tricky prospect for women long trained in the dark arts of self-deprecation. Thirdly, you must face the possibility of rejection. That's the worst one. Women don't like being turned down (we get enough of that in our personal lives), and so, like trial lawyers, we often ask only questions to which we already know the answers. Which means: no risk. Which further means: no reward.

The funny thing is that rejection is not so bad, really. This is something I think men have always understood—that a glorious failure can sometimes be more life affirming than a cautious win. This is why men are constantly asking for stuff they might not even deserve or aren't totally qualified to handle. I don't say this as an insult to men, either; I wish more women would do the same. Because sometimes you get a yes, and even if you weren't prepared for that yes, you rise to the occasion. You aren't ready, and then you are. It's irrational, but it's magical.

I can't instruct you in exactly how to ask for things—it's not my area of expertise, and there are too many variables to account for. Sometimes you have to be gracious and charming, and other times you have to be brash and bold. But generally speaking, it's a surprisingly simple formula: Just freaking *ask*. Because the essential fact is that asking is the best way—the only way, really—to get what you want.

To-Do List,
or Not-to-Do List

Martha Beck

—✳—

On New Year's Eve when I was twenty-one, I had a chat with a friend I'll call Vicky. "The last three months sucked," Vicky said. "I had ten pounds to lose, so I didn't let myself leave my room, except to go to class, until I hit my goal weight." She lifted her champagne. "This is the year I can really start living!" Two days later, Vicky was killed in a traffic accident.

I'm sorry if that story just harshed your mellow. It's been on my mind for decades. Since Vicky's death, I've never been able to stop asking, *How would I spend the next three months if I knew they were my last?* Sitting in a dorm room waiting for my thighs to shrink has never made the list.

Our culture loves the phrase "It's never too late." We want to believe we can toss every adventure onto our bucket lists and accomplish them all. But life is brief. There's a lot we don't have time for.

Chief among them, in my book, is worrying about our bodies—specifically, wishing for completely new ones. You can make alterations, of course. Lose weight, or gain it; have surgeons perform anything from liposuction to mole removal. Ultimately, you'll still have to face the fact that we each get one body per lifetime. The one I'm in now is mine—its puffy little fingers, its strangely shaped skull, its inexorable mortality—and the one you're in is yours. Vicky spent her final months obsessing about her supposed physical imperfections. It's too late for you or me to do the same. Instead, consider this: You have trillions of intricate cells performing a vast array of functions with phenomenal precision, even if you do nothing but suck up pork rinds. That's a *miracle*. So, enough with the self-loathing, already.

And enough, too, with all the things you don't want to do but do anyway to impress people. What a waste! My client Gloria is a physician whose first words to me were, "I hate people, and I hate to touch them." When I asked why she'd chosen such a people-touching profession, she replied, "So I could say I'm a doctor." This is what I call ego candy. The ego's appetite for adulation is endless, its capacity to create genuine happiness nil. It's far too late to spend another minute starving your soul to feed your need for praise.

Nor do you have time for the toxic people you've been trying to turn into healthy ones. Many people become wiser, calmer, and more emotionally healthy with age and experience, while other people display neither psychological health nor interest in changing. You may already have spent much of your life trying to get the love you deserve and need from someone in that second group. I'm so sorry, dear, but it's too late. That love will not be forthcoming.

Here's an idea: How's about you spend less time on relationships in which you feel like Charlie Brown, trying to kick the football Lucy invariably pulls away, and spend more time with people who don't leave you crushed and disappointed over and over and over? Go find the people who are waiting to love you. Because they do exist.

I promise you this: The time you free up can be used in ways you haven't even imagined. Purging your bucket list creates space for all the little things that make up happiness. Like napping, watching television, petting the cat, climbing trees, or solving crosswords. What sane adult has time for such activities, you may ask, when there are so many Important Things to achieve?

Well, I do. I spent years working hard to accomplish Important Things, only to realize that I get limitless joy from filling my bird feeder, reading books about stuff that never happened, and sitting still for hours at a time, not even thinking. Our culture doesn't consider these acceptable alternatives to hard-driving, high-earning Important Thing, yet they're the very activities we turn to once hard work and self-denial have freed up a little time. Think of Vicky. Don't wait. Free that time now.

If someone accuses you of wasting time, tell them that a doctor (that would be me—I have a Ph.D.) has just informed you that you have a fatal condition (life) and don't have long to live (even a hundred years is brief in, say, geologic time). Then go back to learning origami or watching cat videos. It is too late to postpone these things any longer.

We are a time-starved people, obsessed with fitting huge achievements into our few years. In the process, we often fill our buckets with things that don't matter or work. But when we give up on trying to change what can't be changed and simply embrace what we love, a miracle occurs. We notice that the moment to be happy has already arrived. It's here, now.

Contributors

Thelma Adams, a film critic and author of the novel *Playdate*, is at work on her second novel.

Monica Ali's first book, *Brick Lane*, propelled her onto Granta's 2003 list of the "Best of Young British Novelists." She's currently working on her fifth novel.

Katie Arnold-Ratliff, *O, The Oprah Magazine's* articles editor, is the author of the novel *Bright Before Us*.

Christie Aschwanden is an award-winning journalist and essayist whose work has appeared in *The New York Times*, *The Washington Post*, *Slate*, *Smithsonian*, *Discover*, and

Popular Science, among others. She blogs about science at *Last Word On Nothing*.

Dan Baker, Ph.D., is a medical psychologist specializing in stress and cardiovascular disease. His current focus is on advising family-owned businesses.

Celia Barbour, a writer, editor, and cook, lives with her family in a small town on the Hudson River. Her food writing has twice been nominated for a James Beard award.

Martha Beck is a life coach whose most recent book, *The Martha Beck Collection: Essays for Creating Your Right Life, Volume 1,* is an anthology of her work from *O, The Oprah Magazine*, where she's been a columnist since 2001. Beck's other books include *Leaving the Saints, Finding Your Own North Star, The Joy Diet, Steering by Starlight,* and *Finding Your Way in a Wild New World.*

Sister Wendy Beckett is a British hermit and art historian. After teaching for several years, she decided to pursue art. She has authored more than fifteen books on art history, including *The Story of Painting* and *Sister Wendy's American Masterpieces*, and became internationally known for her series of art history documentaries for the BBC.

Amy Bloom, author of the recent novel *Lucky Us*, has written two novels and three collections of short stories, and has been a nominee for both the National Book Award and the National Book Critics Circle Award. She's written for *The New Yorker, The New York Times Magazine*, and *The Atlantic Monthly*, among many other publications. She is currently Wesleyan University's Distinguished Writer in Residence.

Brené Brown, a research professor at the University of Houston, is the author of the *New York Times* #1 bestsellers *Daring Greatly* and *The Gifts of Imperfection*.

Jessica Bruder teaches narrative writing at Columbia University's Graduate School of Journalism and is the author of *Burning Book: A Visual History of Burning Man*.

Veronica Chambers is a prolific author best known for her memoir *Mama's Girl* and the *New York Times* bestseller *Yes, Chef*, coauthored with chef Marcus Samuelsson.

Lisa Congdon is an artist and illustrator and the author of several books, including *Art Inc*; *Whatever You Are, Be a Good One*; *20 Ways to Draw a Tulip*; and *A Collection a Day*.

Heather Greenwood Davis, an award-winning freelance writer, is based in Toronto. Her trip around the world with her husband and two sons earned them the title "Travelers of the Year" from *National Geographic Traveler* magazine in 2012. She is writing a book about the family's experiences.

Pamela Erens is the author of the novels *The Understory*, a *Los Angeles Times* Book Prize finalist, and *The Virgins*, named a Best Book of 2013 by *The New Yorker*, *The New Republic*, *Library Journal*, and *Salon*. Her writing has appeared in *Vogue*, *Elle*, *Glamour*, and *The New York Times*, among other publications. *Reader's Digest* named Erens one of "23 Contemporary Writers You Should Have Read by Now."

Hilene Flanzbaum directs the MFA program at Butler University, where she is a professor of American literature and creative writing. She has published literary criticism, nonfiction, and poetry in journals as varied as *The Yale Journal of Criticism*, *Ploughshares*, and *Tikkun*.

Sue Fliess is a freelance writer and author of eighteen children's books, including *Tons of Trucks*; *Shoes for Me!*; and *Robots, Robots Everywhere!* Her articles have appeared in *The Huffington Post*, *Writer's Digest*, and other publications.

Lise Funderburg is the author of *Pig Candy: Taking My Father South, Taking My Father Home*.

Roxane Gay lives and writes in the Midwest. She is the author of *Ayiti*, *An Untamed State*, *Bad Feminist*, and the forthcoming *Hunger*.

Elizabeth Gilbert is the author of six books of fiction and nonfiction. Her memoir *Eat, Pray, Love* sold more than ten million copies, and her latest novel, *The Signature of All Things*, was named a best book of the year by *Time*, *The New York Times*, and *The Washington Post*.

Marianne Gingher writes fiction and nonfiction and teaches creative writing at the University of North Carolina at Chapel Hill. Her latest memoir, about the writing life, is *Adventures in Pen Land*.

Anne Glusker has swum in pool water, fresh water, and salt water, everywhere from Brooklyn to Morocco. She writes on food, health, education, cultural and gender issues, and whatever else enters her mind while she's swimming.

Lara Kristin Herndon has written about topics ranging from battle cries to baby bottles, and is currently working on a novel. She lives in Connecticut.

Roger Housden is the author of more than twenty books, including the bestselling Ten Poems series. He lives in the Bay Area and runs live and online classes that use writing as a tool to explore the life of the soul.

Joyce Johnson's books include *Minor Characters: A Beat Memoir; Missing Men: A Memoir;* and *The Voice Is All: The Lonely Victory of Jack Kerouac.*

Lila Keary is a New York City–based freelance journalist.

Andrea Lee, an American writer and journalist, lives in Turin, Italy. Her first book, *Russian Journal*, was published in 1981 after portions of it appeared in *The New Yorker*; subsequent books include the novels *Sarah Phillips* and *Lost Hearts in Italy*. Her work has been published in *The New Yorker*, *Vogue*, *W*, *Time*, *Town & Country*, and *The New York Times*, and can be found on her blog, Woman Between the Worlds.

Beth Levine is an award-winning freelance writer who lives in Stamford, Connecticut.

Mark Leyner and his wife divide their time between New York and Los Angeles. His new novel, *Gone with the Mind*, will be published by Little, Brown in 2016.

Valerie Monroe, *O, The Oprah Magazine's* beauty director, is the author of the memoir *In the Weather of the Heart*.

Catherine Newman is the author of the book *Waiting for Birdy* and the blog Ben & Birdy. She lives in Amherst, Massachusetts.

Mary Oliver has written over twenty books of poetry and five collections of essays. Her work has received many awards, including the Pulitzer Prize and the National Book Award. She lives in Hobe Sound, Florida.

Meghan O'Rourke is the author of the poetry collections *Once* and *Halflife*, which was a finalist for both the Patterson Poetry Prize and Britain's Forward Best First Collection prize. Her essays, criticism, and poems have appeared in *Slate, The New Yorker, The New York Times Magazine, The New York Times Book Review, The Nation, Vogue, Poetry, The Kenyon Review,* and *Best American Poetry.* She is currently working on a book about chronic illness.

Catherine Price is the author of two works of nonfiction, *Vitamania: Our Obsessive Quest for Nutritional Perfection* and *101 Places* Not *to See Before You Die.* Her writing has appeared in numerous publications, including *Best American Science Writing, The New York Times, Popular Science, The Los Angeles Times, The San Francisco Chronicle, The Washington Post Magazine,* and *Outside.*

Victoria Redel has published three collections of poetry and four books of fiction. Her work has been widely anthologized and translated into six languages.

Gretchen Reynolds is an award-winning journalist who writes the "Phys Ed" column for *The New York Times* and contributes regularly to *The New York Times Magazine* and other publications.

Robin Romm is the author of a story collection, *The Mother Garden*, and a memoir, *The Mercy Papers*, and is the editor of *Double Bind: Women on Ambition*. She lives in Portland, Oregon.

Jane Smiley's novel *A Thousand Acres* won the Pulitzer Prize and the National Book Critics Circle Award in 1992. Her novel *Horse Heaven* was short-listed for the Orange Prize in 2002, and her novel *Private Life* was chosen as one of the best books of 2010 by *The Atlantic*, *The New Yorker*, and *The Washington Post*. She has written several works of nonfiction, including *Thirteen Ways of Looking at the Novel* and *The Man Who Invented the Computer*. Her new novel is *Some Luck*, the first volume of a trilogy entitled The Last Hundred Years.

Kathryn Sullivan is a former NASA astronaut and was the first American woman to walk in space. In 2004 Sullivan was inducted into the Astronaut Hall of Fame and currently serves as the Under Secretary of Commerce for Oceans and Atmosphere and the National Oceanic and Atmospheric Association Administrator.

Abigail Thomas has written seven books, including, most recently, *What Comes Next and How to Like It*. She teaches writing and lives in Woodstock, New York.

Neil de Grasse Tyson is an award-winning astrophysicist and head of New York City's Hayden Planetarium. His books include *The Sky Is Not the Limit: Adventures of an Urban Astrophysicist*; *Origins: Fourteen Billion Years of Cosmic Evolution*; *Death by Black Hole and Other Cosmic Quandaries*; and *Space Chronicles: Facing the Ultimate Frontier*. Tyson was the executive editor and host of *Cosmos: A Space Time Odyssey*, the twenty-first-century reboot of Carl Sagan's landmark television series.

Justine van der Leun is the author of *Marcus of Umbria: What an Italian Dog Taught an American Girl about Love* and has written for publications including *The New York Observer, Marie Claire, Harper's Magazine*, and *The Bark*.

Patricia Volk is a Guggenheim Fellow and the author of two novels, two memoirs, and two collections of short stories. Her most recent book is *Shocked: My Mother, Schiaparelli, and Me*.

Lauren Winner, an Episcopal priest, is the author of numerous books, including *Still: Notes on a Mid-Faith Crisis* and *Wearing God*. She teaches at Duke Divinity School and lives in Durham, North Carolina.

Jessica Winter is a senior editor at *Slate*.